AF553425

HANDBOOK OF AGRICULTURAL SCIENCE

HANDBOOK OF AGRICULTURAL SCIENCE

By

Dr. H. Shivanna

Professor & Head
Deptt. of Forest Biology & Tree Improvement
College of Forestry
SIRSI, Uttar Kannada
Karnataka (India)

DISCOVERY PUBLISHING HOUSE PVT. LTD
NEW DELHI-110 002

Published by:
Namit Wasan

DISCOVERY PUBLISHING HOUSE PVT. LTD.
4383/4B, Ansari Road, Darya Ganj
New Delhi-110 002 (India)
Phone : +91-11-23279245, 23253475, 43596065
E-mail : discoverypublishinghouse@gmail.com
sales@discoverypublishinggroup.com
web : www.discoverypublishinggroup.com

***Reprinted:* 2019**

***First Published:* 2012**

ISBN: 978-93-5056-004-4

Handbook of Agricultural Science

Printed at:
Infinity Imaging Systems
Delhi

Preface

Agricultural Science is a broad multidisciplinary field that encompasses the parts of exact, natural, economic and social sciences that are used in the practice and understanding of agriculture. (Veterinary Science, but not Animal Science, is often excluded from the definition.)

The two terms are often confused. However, they cover different concepts:

- Agriculture is the set of activities that transform the environment for the production of animals and plants for human use. Agriculture concerns techniques, including the application of agronomic research.
- Agronomy is research and development related to studying and improving plant-based agriculture.

Agricultural sciences include research and development on:

- Production techniques (e.g., irrigation management, recommended nitrogen inputs)

Improving agricultural productivity in terms of quantity and quality (e.g., selection of drought-resistant crops and animals, development of new pesticides, yield-sensing technologies, simulation models of crop growth, *in-vitro* cell culture techniques).

Transformation of primary products into end-consumer products (e.g., production, preservation, and packaging of dairy products).

Prevention and correction of adverse environmental effects (e.g., soil degradation, waste management, bioremediation)

Theoretical production ecology, relating to crop production modelling.

Traditional agricultural systems, sometimes termed subsistence agriculture, which feed most of the poorest people in the world. These systems are of interest as they sometimes retain a level of integration with natural ecological systems greater than that of industrial agriculture, which may be more sustainable than some modern agricultural systems.

As the oldest and largest human intervention in nature, the environmental impact of agriculture in general and more recently intensive agriculture, industrial development, and population growth have raised many questions among agricultural scientists and have led to the development and emergence of new fields. These include technological fields that assume the solution to technological problems lies in better technology, such as integrated pest management, waste treatment technologies, landscape architecture, genomics, and agricultural philosophy fields that include references to food production as something essentially different from non-essential economic 'goods'. In fact, the interaction between these two approaches provide a fertile field for deeper understanding in agricultural science.

Author

Contents

1 Introduction

Agricultural science is a broad multidisciplinary field that encompasses the parts of exact, natural, economic and social sciences that are used in the practice and understanding of agriculture. (Veterinary Science, but not Animal Science, is often excluded from the definition.)

The two terms are often confused. However, they cover different concepts:

- Agriculture is the set of activities that transform the environment for the production of animals and plants for human use. Agriculture concerns techniques, including the application of agronomic research.
- Agronomy is research and development related to studying and improving plant-based agriculture.

Agricultural Sciences include research and development on:

- Production techniques (e.g., irrigation management, recommended nitrogen inputs)
- Improving agricultural productivity in terms of quantity and quality (e.g., selection of drought-resistant crops and animals, development of new pesticides, yield-sensing technologies, simulation models of crop growth, *in vitro* cell culture techniques)

Transformation of primary products into end-consumer products (e.g., production, preservation, and packaging of dairy products).

Prevention and correction of adverse environmental effects (e.g., soil degradation, waste management, bioremediation)

Theoretical production ecology, relating to crop production modelling.

Traditional agricultural systems, sometimes termed subsistence agriculture, which feed most of the poorest people in the world. These systems are of interest as they sometimes retain a level of integration with natural ecological systems greater than that of industrial agriculture, which may be more sustainable than some modern agricultural systems.

Food production and demand on a global basis, with special attention paid to the major producers, such as China, India, Brazil and the USA.

Agricultural Science: A Local Science

With the exception of theoretical agronomy, research in agronomy, more than in any other field, is strongly related to local areas. It can be considered a science of ecoregions, because it is closely linked to soil properties and climate, which are never exactly the same from one place to another. Many people think an agricultural production system relying on local weather, soil characteristics, and specific crops has to be studied locally. Others feel a need to know and understand production systems in as many areas as possible, and the human dimension of interaction with nature.

History of Agricultural Science

Agricultural science began with Gregor Mendel's genetic work, but in modern terms might be better dated from the chemical fertilizer outputs of plant physiological understanding in eighteenth century Germany. In the United States, a scientific revolution in agriculture began with the Hatch Act of 1887, which used the term 'agricultural science'. The Hatch Act was driven by farmers' interest in knowing the constituents of early artificial fertilizer. The Smith-Hughes Act of 1917 shifted agricultural education back to its vocational roots, but the scientific foundation had been built. After 1906, public expenditures on agricultural research in the US exceeded private expenditures for the next 44 years.

Intensification of agriculture since the 1960s in developed and developing countries, often referred to as the Green Revolution, was closely tied to progress made in selecting and improving crops and animals for high productivity, as well as to developing additional inputs such as artificial fertilizers and phytosanitary products.

As the oldest and largest human intervention in nature, the environmental impact of agriculture in general and more recently intensive agriculture, industrial development, and population growth have raised many questions among agricultural scientists and have led to the development and emergence of new fields. These include technological fields that assume the solution to technological problems lies in better technology, such as integrated pest management, waste treatment technologies, landscape architecture, genomics, and agricultural philosophy fields that include references to food production as something essentially different from non-essential economic 'goods'. In fact, the interaction between these two approaches provide a fertile field for deeper understanding in agricultural science.

New technologies, such as biotechnology and computer science (for data processing and storage), and technological advances have made it possible to develop new research fields, including genetic engineering, agrophysics, improved statistical analysis, and precision farming. Balancing these, as above, are the natural and human sciences of agricultural science that seek to understand the human-nature interactions of traditional agriculture, including interaction of religion and agriculture, and the non-material components of agricultural production systems.

Agriculture sciences seek to feed the world's population while preventing biosafety problems that may affect human health and the environment. This requires promoting good management of natural resources and respect for the environment, and increasingly concern for the psychological well-being of all concerned in the food production and consumption system.

Economic, environmental, and social aspects of agriculture sciences are subjects of ongoing debate. Recent crises (such as avian influenza, mad cow disease and issues such as the use of genetically modified organisms) illustrate the complexity and importance of this debate.

2 Intensive Farming

Intensive farming or intensive agriculture is an agricultural production system characterized by the high inputs of capital, labour, or heavy usage of technologies such as pesticides and chemical fertilizers relative to land area.

This is in contrast to many forms of sustainable agriculture such as organic farming or extensive agriculture, which involve a relatively low input of materials and labour, relative to the area of land farmed, and which focus on maintaining long-term ecological health of farmland, so that it can be farmed indefinitely.

Modern day forms of intensive crop-based agriculture involve the use of mechanical ploughing, chemical fertilizers, plant growth regulators and/or pesticides. It is associated with the increasing use of agricultural mechanization, which have enabled a substantial increase in production, yet have also dramatically increased environmental pollution by increasing erosion and poisoning water with agricultural chemicals.

Intensive animal farming practices can involve very large numbers of animals raised on limited land which require large amounts of food, water and medical inputs (required to keep the animals healthy in cramped conditions). Very large or confined indoor intensive livestock operations (particularly descriptive of common US farming practices) are often referred to as Factory farming and are criticised by opponents for the low level of animal welfare standards and associated pollution and health issues.

Intensive agriculture has numbers of benefits:

- Significantly increased yield per acre, per person, and per dollar relative to extensive farming and therefore,
- Food becomes more affordable to the consumer as it costs less to produce.
- The same area of land is able to supply food and fibre for a larger population reducing the risk of starvation.

Intensive farming alters the environment in many ways.

Limits or destroys the natural habitat of most wild creatures, and leads to soil erosion.

Use of fertilizers can alter the biology of rivers and lakes. Some environmentalists attribute the hypoxic zone in the Gulf of Mexico as being encouraged by nitrogen fertilization of the algae bloom.

Pesticides generally kill useful insects as well as those that destroy crops.

Is often not sustainable if not properly managed — may result in desertification, or land that is so poisonous and eroded that nothing else will grow there.

Requires large amounts of energy input to produce, transport, and apply chemical fertilizers/pesticides

The chemicals used may leave the field as runoff eventually ending up in rivers and lakes or may drain into groundwater aquifers.

Use of pesticides have numerous negative health effects in workers who apply them, people that live nearby the area of application or downstream/downwind from it, and consumers who eat the pesticides which remain on their food.

Oysters were likely the first sea animal to be transported from one area to another and cultivated as food. The ancient world, while knowing little about the reproduction of oysters, knew much about the conditions necessary for their growth. Pliny the Elder, a noted Roman naturalist of the first century, left an account of artificial oyster beds established in Lake Lucrinus near Naples by a Sergius Orata about 95 B.C. Orata's methods consisted of preparing the grounds by removing other forms of marine life, planting seed oysters, cultivating the oysters by keeping them separated in order to grow to a well-formed, mature size, and finally harvesting them when they were ready for market. Modern oyster farming, based on the knowledge of oyster biology, basically follows the Roman procedure. Fisheries and Oceans Canada article *American Oyster*

Terrace

In agriculture, a terrace is a levelled section of a hilly cultivated area, designed as a method of soil conservation to slow or prevent the rapid surface runoff of irrigation water. Often such land is formed into multiple terraces, giving a stepped appearance. The human landscapes of rice cultivation in terraces that follow the natural contours of the escarpments like contour ploughing is a classic feature of the island of Bali and the Banaue Rice Terraces in Benguet, Philippines. In Peru, the Inca made use of otherwise unusable slopes by drystone walling to create terraces.

A paddy field is a flooded parcel of arable land used for growing rice and other semiaquatic crops. Paddy fields are a typical feature of rice-growing countries of east and southeast Asia including Malaysia, China, Sri Lanka, Myanmar, Thailand, Korea, Japan, Vietnam, Taiwan,

Indonesia, India, and the Philippines. They are also found in other rice-growing regions such as Piedmont (Italy), the Camargue (France) and the Artibonite Valley (Haiti). They can occur naturally along rivers or marshes, or can be constructed, even on hillsides, often with much labour and materials. They require large quantities of water for irrigation, which can be quite complex for a highly developed system of paddy fields. Flooding provides water essential to the growth of the crop. It also gives an environment favourable to the strain of rice being grown, and is hostile to many species of weeds. As the only draft animal species which is adapted for life in wetlands, the water buffalo is in widespread use in Asian rice paddies. There are significant adverse environmental impacts from rice paddy cultivation due to the generation of large quantities of methane gas. World methane production due to rice paddies has been estimated in the range of 50 to 100 million tonnes per annum; this level of greenhouse gas generation is a large component of the global warming threat and derives simply from an expanding human population.

Rice-farming and the use of paddies in Korea is ancient. Korean paddy-farming can provide cultural background on the use of paddies in East Asia. A pit-house at the Daecheon-ni site yielded carbonized rice grains and radiocarbon dates indicating that rice cultivation may have begun as early as the Middle Jeulmun Pottery Period in the Korean Peninsula. The earliest rice cultivation in the Korean Peninsula may have used dry-fields instead of paddies.

The earliest Mumun features were usually located in low-lying narrow gulleys that were naturally swampy and fed by the local stream system. Some Mumun paddies in flat areas were made of a series of squares and rectangles separated by bunds approximately 10 cm in height, while terraced paddies consisted of long irregularly shapes that followed natural contours of the land at various levels.

Mumun Period rice farmers used all of the elements that are present in today's paddies such terracing, bunds, canals, and small reservoirs. We can grasp some paddy-farming techniques of the Middle Mumun from the well-preserved wooden tools excavated from archaeological rice paddies at the Majeon-ni Site. However, iron tools for paddy-farming were not introduced until sometime after 200 B.C. The spatial scale of individual paddies, and thus entire paddy-fields, increased with the regular use of iron tools in the Three Kingdoms of Korea Period.

Modern Intensive Farming Types

Modern intensive farming refers to the industrialized production of animals (livestock, poultry and fish) and crops. The methods deployed are designed to produce the highest output at the lowest cost; usually using economies of scale, modern machinery, modern medicine, and global trade for financing, purchases and sales. The practice is widespread in developed nations, and most of the meat, dairy, eggs, and crops available in supermarkets are produced in this manner.

Sustainable Intensive Farming

Biointensive agriculture focuses on maximizing efficiency: yield per unit area, yield per energy input, yield per water input, etc. Agroforestry combines agriculture and orchard/forestry technologies to create more integrated, diverse, productive, profitable, healthy and sustainable land-use systems. Intercropping can also increase total yields per unit of area or reduce inputs to achieve the same, and thus represents (potentially sustainable) agricultural intensification. Unfortunately, bra's of any specific crop often diminish and the change can present new challenges to farmers relying on modern farming equipment which is best suited to monoculture. Vertical farming, a type of intensive crop production that would grow food on a large scale in urban centers, has been proposed as a way to reduce the negative environmental impact of traditional rural agriculture.

Intensive Aquaculture

Aquaculture is the cultivation of the natural produce of water (fish, shellfish, algae, seaweed and other aquatic organisms). Intensive Aquaculture can often involve tanks or other highly controlled systems which are designed to boost production for the available volume or area of water resource.

Intensive Livestock Farming

The modern examples of intensive farming are broadly referred to as Concentrated Animal Feeding Operations (CAFOs) or often termed Factory farming. These include:

- Intensive pig farming or Intensive piggery farming
- Large scale chicken farms
- Cattle feed lots

Managed Intensive Grazing

This sustainable intensive livestock management system is increasingly used to optimize production within a sustainability framework and is generally not considered Factory farming. Intensive farming or intensive agriculture is an agricultural production system characterized by the high inputs of capital, labour, or heavy usage of technologies such as pesticides and chemical fertilizers relative to land area.

This is in contrast to many forms of sustainable agriculture such as permaculture or extensive agriculture, which involve a relatively low input of materials and labour, relative to the area of land farmed, and which focus on maintaining long-term ecological health of farmland, so that it can be farmed indefinitely.

Modern day forms of intensive crop based agriculture involve the use of mechanical ploughing, chemical fertilizers, herbicides, fungicides, insecticides, plant growth regulators and/or pesticides. It is associated with the increasing use of agricultural mechanization, which have enabled a substantial increase in production, yet have also dramatically increased environmental pollution by increasing erosion, poisoning water with agricultural chemicals, and destroying forests to make room for farmland.

Intensive animal farming practices can involve very large numbers of animals raised on limited land which require large amounts of food, water and medical inputs (required to keep the animals healthy in cramped conditions). Very large or confined indoor intensive livestock operations (particularly descriptive of common US farming practices) are often referred to as Factory farming and are criticised by opponents for the low level of animal welfare standards and associated pollution and health issues.

Individual Industrial Agriculture Farm

Major challenges and issues faced by individual industrial agriculture farms include:

- integrated farming systems;
- crop sequencing;
- water use efficiency;
- nutrient audits;
- herbicide resistance;
- financial instruments (such as futures and options);
- collect and understand own farm information;
- knowing your products;
- knowing your markets;
- knowing your customers;
- satisfying customer needs;

- securing an acceptable profit margin;
- cost of servicing debt;
- ability to earn and access off-farm income;
- management of machinery and stewardship investments.

Integrated Farming Systems

An integrated farming system is a progressive biologically integrated sustainable agriculture system such as Integrated Multi-Trophic Aquaculture or Zero waste agriculture whose implementation requires exacting knowledge of the interactions of numerous species and whose benefits include sustainability and increased profitability.

Elements of this integration can include:

- Intentionally introducing flowering plants into agricultural ecosystems to increase pollen-and nectar-resources required by natural enemies of insect pests

Crop Rotation

Satellite image of circular crop fields in Haskell County, Kansas in late June 2001. Healthy, growing crops of corn and sorghum are green (Sorghum may be slightly paler). Wheat is brilliant gold. Fields of brown have been recently harvested and plowed under or have lain in fallow for the year.

Crop rotation or crop sequencing is the practice of growing a series of dissimilar types of crops in the same space in sequential seasons for various benefits such as to avoid the build up of pathogens and pests that often occurs when one species is continuously cropped. Crop rotation also seeks to balance the fertility demands of various crops to avoid excessive depletion of soil nutrients. A traditional component of crop rotation is the replenishment of nitrogen through the use of green manure in sequence with cereals and other crops. It is one component of polyculture. Crop rotation can also improve soil structure and fertility by alternating deep-rooted and shallow-rooted plants.

Crop irrigation accounts for 70 per cent of the world's fresh water use. The agricultural sector of most countries is important both economically and politically, and water subsidies are common. Conservation advocates have urged removal of all subsidies to force farmers to grow more water-efficient crops and adopt less wasteful irrigation techniques.

Optimal water efficiency means minimizing losses due to evaporation, runoff or subsurface drainage. An evaporation pan can be used to determine how much water is required to irrigate the land. Flood irrigation, the oldest and most common type, is often very uneven in distribution, as parts of a field may receive excess water in order to deliver sufficient quantities to other parts. Overhead irrigation, using center-pivot or lateral-moving sprinklers, gives a much more equal and controlled distribution pattern. Drip irrigation is the most expensive and least-used type, but offers the best results in delivering water to plant roots with minimal losses.

As changing irrigation systems can be a costly undertaking, conservation efforts often concentrate on maximizing the efficiency of the existing system. This may include chiseling compacted soils, creating furrow dikes to prevent runoff, and using soil moisture and rainfall sensors to optimize irrigation schedules.

Water catchment management measures include recharge pits, which capture rainwater and runoff and use it to recharge ground water supplies. This helps in the formation of ground water wells etc. and eventually reduces soil erosion caused due to running water.

Nutrient Audits

Better nutrient audits allow farmers to spend less money on nutrients and to create less pollution since less nutrient is added to the soil and thus there is less to run off and pollute. Methodologies for assessing soil nutrient balances have been studied and used for farms and entire countries for decades. But at present "there is no standard methodology for calculating nutrient budgets and there are no accepted 'benchmarks' figures against which to assess farm nutrient use efficiency. *A standard methodology* for calculating nutrient budgets on farms diffuse water and air pollution from agriculture *through* best management practices in the use of fertilisers and organic manures, as part of the continued development of economically and environmentally sustainable farming systems."

Herbicide Resistance

In agriculture large scale and systematic weeding is usually required, often performed by machines such as cultivators or liquid herbicide sprayers. Selective herbicides kill specific targets while leaving the desired crop relatively unharmed. Some of these act by interfering with the growth of the weed and are often based on plant hormones. Weed control through herbicide is made more difficult when the weeds become resistant to the herbicide. Solutions include:

- using cover crops (especially those with allopathic properties) that out-compete weeds and/or inhibit their regeneration;
- using a different herbicide;
- using a different crop (e.g. genetically altered to be herbicide resistant; which ironically can create herbicide resistant weeds through horizontal gene transfer);
- using a different variety (e.g. locally-adapted variety that resists, tolerates, or even out-competes weeds);
- ploughing;
- ground cover such as mulch or plastic;
- manual removal.

3 Agriculture

Agriculture is the production of food and goods through farming. Agriculture was the key development that led to the rise of human civilization, with the husbandry of domesticated animals and plants (i.e. crops) creating food surpluses that enabled the development of more densely populated and stratified societies. The study of agriculture is known as agricultural science. Central to human society, agriculture is also observed in certain species of ant and termite.

Agriculture encompasses a wide variety of specialties and techniques, including ways to expand the lands suitable for plant raising, by digging water-channels and other forms of irrigation. Cultivation of crops on arable land and the pastoral herding of livestock on rangeland remain at the foundation of agriculture. In the past century there has been increasing concern to identify and quantify various forms of agriculture. In the developed world the range usually extends between sustainable agriculture (e.g. permaculture or organic agriculture) and intensive farming (e.g. industrial agriculture).

Modern agronomy, plant breeding, pesticides and fertilizers, and technological improvements have sharply increased yields from cultivation, and at the same time have caused widespread ecological damage and negative human health effects. Selective breeding and modern practices in animal husbandry such as intensive pig farming (and similar practices applied to the chicken) have similarly increased the output of meat, but have raised concerns about animal cruelty and the health effects of the antibiotics, growth hormones, and other chemicals commonly used in industrial meat production.

The major agricultural products can be broadly grouped into foods, fibers, fuels, and raw materials. In the 2000s, plants have been used to grow biofuels, biopharmaceuticals, bioplastics, and pharmaceuticals. Specific foods include cereals, vegetables, fruits, and meat. Fibers include cotton, wool, hemp, silk and flax. Raw materials include lumber and bamboo. Other useful materials are produced by plants, such as resins. Biofuels include methane from biomass, ethanol, and biodiesel. Cut flowers, nursery plants, tropical fish and birds for the pet trade are some of the ornamental products.

In 2007, about one third of the world's workers were employed in agriculture. The services sector has overtaken agriculture as the economic sector employing the most people worldwide. Despite the size of its workforce, agricultural production accounts for less than five per cent of the gross world product (an aggregate of all gross domestic products).

Agriculture has played a key role in the development of human civilization. Until the Industrial Revolution, the vast majority of the human population laboured in agriculture. Development of agricultural techniques has steadily increased agricultural productivity, and the widespread diffusion of these techniques during a time period is often called an agricultural revolution. A remarkable shift in agricultural practices has occurred over the past century in response to new technologies. In particular, the Haber-Bosch method for synthesizing ammonium nitrate made the traditional practice of recycling nutrients with crop rotation and animal manure less necessary.

Synthetic nitrogen, along with mined rock phosphate, pesticides and mechanization, have greatly increased crop yields in the early 20th century. Increased supply of grains has led to cheaper livestock as well. Further, global yield increases were experienced later in the 20th century when high-yield varieties of common staple grains such as rice, wheat, and corn (maize) were introduced as a part of the Green Revolution. The Green Revolution exported the technologies (including pesticides and synthetic nitrogen) of the developed world to the developing world. Thomas Malthus famously predicted that the Earth would not be able to support its growing population, but technologies such as the Green Revolution have allowed the world to produce a surplus of food.

Many governments have subsidized agriculture to ensure an adequate food supply. These agricultural subsidies are often linked to the production of certain commodities such as wheat, corn (maize), rice, soybeans, and milk. These subsidies, especially when instituted by developed countries have been noted as protectionist, inefficient, and environmentally damaging. In the past century agriculture has been characterized by enhanced productivity, the use of synthetic fertilizers and pesticides, selective breeding, mechanization, water contamination, and farm subsidies. Proponents of organic farming such as Sir Albert Howard argued in the early 1900s that the overuse of pesticides and synthetic fertilizers damages the long-term fertility of the soil. While this feeling lay dormant for decades, as environmental awareness has increased in the 2000s there has been a movement towards sustainable agriculture by some farmers, consumers, and policymakers. In recent years there has been a backlash against perceived external environmental effects of mainstream agriculture, particularly regarding water pollution, resulting in the organic movement. One of the major forces behind this movement has been the European Union, which first certified organic food in 1991 and began reform of its Common Agricultural Policy (CAP) in 2005 to phase out commodity-linked farm subsidies, also known as decoupling. The growth of organic farming has renewed research in alternative technologies such as integrated pest management and selective breeding. Recent mainstream technological developments include genetically modified food.

In late 2007, several factors pushed up the price of grains consumed by humans as well as used to feed poultry and dairy cows and other cattle, causing higher prices of wheat (up 58%), soybean (up 32%), and maize (up 11%) over the year. Food riots took place in several countries across the world. Contributing factors included drought in Australia and elsewhere, increasing demand for grain-fed animal products from the growing middle classes of countries such as China and India, diversion of foodgrain to biofuel production and trade restrictions imposed by several countries.

An epidemic of stem rust on wheat caused by race Ug99 is currently spreading across Africa and into Asia and is causing major concern. Approximately 40 per cent of the world's agricultural land is seriously degraded. In Africa, if current trends of soil degradation continue, the continent might be able to feed just 25 per cent of its population by 2025, according to UNU's Ghana-based Institute for Natural Resources in Africa.

Since its development roughly 10,000 years ago, agriculture has expanded vastly in geographical coverage and yields. Throughout this expansion, new technologies and new crops were integrated. Even then crops were modified through cross-breeding for better yields. Agricultural practices such as irrigation, crop rotation, fertilizers, and pesticides were developed long ago, but have made great strides in the past century. The history of agriculture has played a major role in human history, as agricultural progress has been a crucial factor in worldwide socio-economic change. Wealth-concentration and militaristic specializations rarely seen in hunter-gatherer cultures are commonplace in societies which practice agriculture. So, too, are arts such as epic literature and monumental architecture, as well as codified legal systems. When farmers became capable of producing food beyond the needs of their own families, others in their society were freed to devote themselves to projects other than food acquisition. Historians and anthropologists have long argued that the development of agriculture made civilization possible.

The Fertile Crescent of Western Asia, Egypt, and India were sites of the earliest planned sowing and harvesting of plants that had previously been gathered in the wild. Independent development of agriculture occurred in northern and southern China, Africa's Sahel, New Guinea and several regions of the Americas. The eight so-called Neolithic founder crops of agriculture appear: first emmer wheat and einkorn wheat, then hulled barley, peas, lentils, bitter vetch, chick peas and flax.

By 7000 BC, small-scale agriculture reached Egypt. From at least 7000 BC the Indian subcontinent saw farming of wheat and barley, as attested by archaeological excavation at Mehrgarh in Balochistan. By 6000 BC, mid-scale farming was entrenched on the banks of the Nile. About this time, agriculture was developed independently in the Far East, with rice, rather than wheat, as the primary crop. Chinese and Indonesian farmers went on to domesticate taro and beans including mung, soy and azuki. To complement these new sources of carbohydrates, highly organized net fishing of rivers, lakes and ocean shores in these areas brought in great volumes of essential protein. Collectively, these new methods of farming and fishing inaugurated a human population boom that dwarfed all previous expansions and continues today.

By 5000 BC, the Sumerians had developed core agricultural techniques including large-scale intensive cultivation of land, mono-cropping, organized irrigation, and the use of a specialized labour force, particularly along the waterway now known as the Shatt al-Arab, from its Persian Gulf delta to the confluence of the Tigris and Euphrates. Domestication of wild aurochs and mouflon into cattle and sheep, respectively, ushered in the large-scale use of animals for food/fiber and as beasts of burden. The shepherd joined the farmer as an essential provider for sedentary and semi-nomadic societies. Maize, manioc, and arrowroot were first domesticated in the Americas as far back as 5200 BC. The potato, tomato, pepper, squash, several varieties of bean, tobacco, and several other plants were also developed in the New World, as was extensive terracing of steep hillsides in much of Andean South America. The Greeks and Romans built on techniques pioneered by the Sumerians but made few fundamentally new advances. Southern Greeks struggled with very poor soils, yet managed to become a dominant society for years. The Romans were noted for an emphasis on the cultivation of crops for trade.

During the Middle Ages, farmers in North Africa, the Near East, and Europe began making use of agricultural technologies including irrigation systems based on hydraulic and hydrostatic principles, machines such as norias, water-raising machines, dams, and reservoirs. This combined with the invention of a three-field system of crop rotation and the moldboard plow greatly improved agricultural efficiency.

Infrared image of the farm. To the untrained eye, this image appears a hodge-podge of colours without any apparent purpose. But farmers are now trained to see yellows where crops are infested, shades of red indicating crop health, black where flooding occurs, and brown where unwanted pesticides land on chemical-free crops.

After 1492, a global exchange of previously local crops and livestock breeds occurred. Key crops involved in this exchange included the tomato, maize, potato, manioc, cocoa bean and tobacco going from the New World to the Old, and several varieties of wheat, spices, coffee, and sugar cane going from the Old World to the New. The most important animal exportation from the Old World to the New were those of the horse and dog (dogs were already present in the pre-Columbian Americas but not in the numbers and breeds suited to farm work). Although not usually food animals, the horse (including donkeys and ponies) and dog quickly filled essential production roles on western-hemisphere farms.

The potato became an important staple crop in northern Europe. Since being introduced by Portuguese in the 16th century, maize and manioc have replaced traditional African crops as the continent's most important staple food crops.

By the early 1800s, agricultural techniques, implements, seed stocks and cultivated plants selected and given a unique name because of its decorative or useful characteristics had so improved that yield per land unit was many times that seen in the Middle Ages. With the rapid rise of mechanization in the late 19th and 20th centuries, particularly in the form of the tractor, farming tasks could be done with a speed and on a scale previously impossible. These advances have led to efficiencies enabling certain modern farms in the United States, Argentina, Israel, Germany, and a few other nations to output volumes of high-quality produce per land unit at what may be the practical limit. The Haber-Bosch method for synthesizing ammonium nitrate represented a major breakthrough and allowed crop yields to overcome previous constraints. In the past century agriculture has been characterized by enhanced productivity, the substitution of labour for synthetic fertilizers and pesticides, water pollution, and farm subsidies. In recent years there has been a backlash against the external environmental effects of conventional agriculture, resulting in the organic movement.

The cereals rice, corn, and wheat provide 60 per cent of human food supply. Between 1700 and 1980, "the total area of cultivated land worldwide increased 466 per cent" and yields increased dramatically, particularly because of selectively-bred high-yielding varieties, fertilizers, pesticides, irrigation, and machinery. For example, irrigation increased corn yields in eastern Colorado by 400 to 500 per cent from 1940 to 1997.

However, concerns have been raised over the sustainability of intensive agriculture. Intensive agriculture has become associated with decreased soil quality in India and Asia, and there has been increased concern over the effects of fertilizers and pesticides on the environment, particularly as population increases and food demand expands. The monocultures typically used in intensive agriculture increase the number of pests, which are controlled through pesticides. Integrated pest management (IPM), which "has been promoted for decades and has had some notable successes" has not significantly affected the use of pesticides because policies encourage the use of pesticides and IPM is knowledge-intensive. Although the 'Green Revolution' significantly increased rice yields in Asia, yield increases have not occurred in the past 15-20 years. The genetic 'yield potential' has increased for wheat, but the yield potential for rice has not increased since 1966, and the yield potential for maize has 'barely increased in 35 years'.

It takes a decade or two for herbicide-resistant weeds to emerge, and insects become resistant to insecticides within about a decade. Crop rotation helps to prevent resistances.

Agricultural exploration expeditions, since the late nineteenth century, have been mounted to find new species and new agricultural practices in different areas of the world. Two early examples of expeditions include Frank N. Meyer's fruit-and nut-collecting trip to China and Japan from 1916-1918 and the Dorsett-Morse Oriental Agricultural Exploration Expedition to China, Japan, and Korea from 1929-1931 to collect soybean germplasm to support the rise in soybean agriculture in the United States.

In 2005, the agricultural output of China was the largest in the world, accounting for almost one-sixth of world share, followed by the EU, India and the USA, according to the International Monetary Fund. More than 40 million Chinese farmers have been displaced from their land in recent years, usually for economic development, contributing to the 87,000 demonstrations and riots across China in 2005. Economists measure the total factor productivity of agriculture and by this measure agriculture in the United States is roughly 2.6 times more productive than it was in 1948.

Six countries — the United States; Canada; France; Australia; Argentina and Thailand — supply 90 per cent of grain exports. The United States controls almost half of world grain exports. Water deficits, which are already spurring heavy grain imports in numerous middle-sized countries, including Algeria, Iran, Egypt, and Mexico, may soon do the same in larger countries, such as China or India.

Crop Production Systems

Cropping systems vary among farms depending on the available resources and constraints, geography and climate of the farm' government policy' economic, social and political pressures and the philosophy and culture of the farmer.Shifting cultivation (or slash and burn) is a system in which forests are burnt, releasing nutrients to support cultivation of annual and then perennial crops for a period of several years. Then the plot is left fallow to regrow forest, and the farmer moves to a new plot, returning after many more years (10-20). This fallow period is shortened if population density grows, requiring the input of nutrients (fertilizer or manure) and some manual pest control. Annual cultivation is the next phase of intensity in which there is no fallow period. This requires even greater nutrient and pest control inputs. Further industrialization lead to the use of monocultures, when one cultivar is planted on a large acreage.Because of the low biodiversity, nutrient use is uniform and pests tend to build up, necessitating the greater use of pesticides and fertilizers. Multiple cropping, in which several crops are grown sequentially in one year, and intercropping, when several crops are grown at the same time are other kinds of annual cropping systems known as polycultures.

In tropical environments, all of these cropping systems are practiced. In subtropical and arid environments, the timing and extent of agriculture may be limited by rainfall, either not allowing multiple annual crops in a year, or requiring irrigation. In all of these environments perennial crops are grown (coffee, chocolate) and systems are practiced such as agroforestry. In temperate environments, where ecosystems were predominantly grassland or prairie, highly productive annual cropping is the dominant farming system.

The last century has seen the intensification, concentration and specialization of agriculture, relying upon new technologies of agricultural chemicals (fertilizers and pesticides), mechanization, and plant breeding (hybrids and GMO's). In the past few decades, a move towards sustainability in agriculture has also developed, integrating ideas of socio-economic justice and conservation of resources and the environment within a farming system. This has led to the development of many responses to the conventional agriculture approach, including organic agriculture, urban agriculture, community supported agriculture, ecological or biological agriculture, integrated farming and holistic management, as well as an increased trend towards agricultural diversification.

Animals, including horses, mules, oxen, camels, llamas, alpacas, and dogs, are often used to help cultivate fields, harvest crops, wrangle other animals, and transport farm products to buyers. Animal husbandry not only refers to the breeding and raising of animals for meat or to harvest animal products (like milk, eggs, or wool) on a continual basis, but also to the breeding and care of species for work and companionship. Livestock production systems can be defined based on feed source, as grassland-based, mixed, and landless. Grassland based livestock production relies upon plant material such as shrubland, rangeland, and pastures for feeding ruminant animals. Outside nutrient inputs may be used, however manure is returned directly to the grassland as a major nutrient source. This system is particularly important in areas where crop production is not feasible because of climate or soil, representing 30-40 million pastoralists. Mixed production systems use grassland, fodder crops and grain feed crops as feed for ruminant and monogastic (one stomach; mainly chickens and pigs) livestock. Manure is typically recycled in mixed systems as a fertilizer for crops. Approximately 68 per cent of all agricultural land is permanent pastures used in the production of livestock. Landless systems rely upon feed from outside the farm, representing the de-linking of crop and livestock production found more prevalently in OECD member countries. In the U.S., 70 per cent of the grain grown is fed to animals on feedlots. Synthetic fertilizers are more heavily relied upon for crop production and manure utilization becomes a challenge as well as a source for pollution.

Tillage is the practice of plowing soil to prepare for planting or for nutrient incorporation or for pest control. Tillage varies in intensity from conventional to no-till. It may improve productivity by warming the soil, incorporating fertilizer and controlling weeds, but also renders soil more prone to erosion, triggers the decomposition of organic matter releasing CO_2 and reduces the abundance and diversity of soil organisms.

Pest control includes the management of weeds, insects/ mites, and diseases. Chemical (pesticides), biological (biocontrol), mechanical (tillage), and cultural practices are used. Cultural practices include crop rotation, culling, cover crops, intercropping, composting, avoidance, and resistance. Integrated pest management attempts to use all of these methods to keep pest populations below the number which would cause economic loss, and recommends pesticides as a last resort.

Nutrient management includes both the source of nutrient inputs for crop and livestock production, and the method of utilization of manure produced by livestock. Nutrient inputs can be chemical inorganic fertilizers, manure, green manure, compost and mined minerals. Crop nutrient use may also be managed using cultural techniques such as crop rotation or a fallow period. Manure is used either by holding livestock where the feed crop is growing, such as in managed intensive rotational grazing, or by spreading either dry or liquid formulations of manure on cropland or pastures.

Water management is where rainfall is insufficient or variable, which occurs to some degree in most regions of the world. Some farmers use irrigation to supplement rainfall. In other areas such as the Great Plains in the U.S. and Canada, farmers use a fallow year to conserve soil moisture to use for growing a crop in the following year. Agriculture represents 70 per cent of freshwater use worldwide.

In the United States, food costs attributed to processing, distribution, and marketing have risen while the costs attributed to farming have declined. This is related to the greater efficiency of farming, combined with the increased level of value addition (e.g. more highly processed products) provided by the supply chain. From 1960 to 1980 the farm share was around 40 per cent, but by 1990 it had declined to 30 per cent and by 1998, 22.2 per cent. Market concentration has increased in the sector as well, with the top 20 food manufacturers accounting for half the food-processing value in 1995, over double that produced in 1954. As of 2000 the top six US supermarket groups had 50 per cent of sales compared to 32 per cent in 1992. Although the total effect of the increased market concentration is likely increased efficiency, the changes redistribute economic surplus from producers (farmers) and consumers, and may have negative implications for rural communities.

Crop alteration has been practiced by humankind for thousands of years, since the beginning of civilization. Altering crops through breeding practices changes the genetic make-up of a plant to develop crops with more beneficial characteristics for humans, for example, larger fruits or seeds, drought-tolerance, or resistance to pests. Significant advances in plant breeding ensued after the work of geneticist Gregor Mendel. His work on dominant and recessive alleles gave plant breeders a better understanding of genetics and brought great insights to the techniques utilized by plant breeders. Crop breeding includes techniques such as plant selection with desirable traits, self-pollination and cross-pollination, and molecular techniques that genetically modify the organism. Domestication of plants has, over the centuries increased yield, improved disease resistance and drought tolerance, eased harvest and improved the taste and nutritional value of crop plants. Careful selection and breeding have had enormous effects on the characteristics of crop plants. Plant selection and breeding in the 1920s and 1930s improved pasture (grasses and clover) in New Zealand. Extensive

X-ray an ultraviolet induced mutagenesis efforts (i.e. primitive genetic engineering) during the 1950s produced the modern commercial varieties of grains such as wheat, corn (maize) and barley.

The green revolution popularized the use of conventional hybridization to increase yield many folds by creating 'high-yielding varieties'. For example, average yields of corn (maize) in the USA have increased from around 2.5 tons per hectare (t/ha) (40 bushels per acre) in 1900 to about 9.4 t/ha (150 bushels per acre) in 2001. Similarly, worldwide average wheat yields have increased from less than 1 t/ha in 1900 to more than 2.5 t/ha in 1990. South American average wheat yields are around 2 t/ha, African under 1 t/ha, Egypt and Arabia up to 3.5 to 4 t/ha with irrigation. In contrast, the average wheat yield in countries such as France is over 8 t/ha. Variations in yields are due mainly to variation in climate, genetics, and the level of intensive farming techniques (use of fertilizers, chemical pest control, growth control to avoid lodging).

Genetically Modified Organisms (GMO) are organisms whose genetic material has been altered by genetic engineering techniques generally known as recombinant DNA technology. Genetic engineering has expanded the genes available to breeders to utilize in creating desired germlines for new crops. After mechanical tomato-harvesters were developed in the early 1960s, agricultural scientists genetically modified tomatoes to be more resistant to mechanical handling. More recently, genetic engineering is being employed in various parts of the world, to create crops with other beneficial traits.

Roundup-Ready seed has a herbicide resistant gene implanted into its genome that allows the plants to tolerate exposure to glyphosate. Roundup is a trade name for a glyphosate based product, which is a systemic, non-selective herbicide used to kill weeds. Roundup-ready seeds allow the farmer to grow a crop that can be sprayed with glyphosate to control weeds without harming the resistant crop. Herbicide-tolerant crops are used by farmers worldwide. Today, 92 per cent of soybean acreage in the US is planted with genetically-modified herbicide-tolerant plants. With the increasing use of herbicide-tolerant crops, comes an increase in the use of glyphosate-based herbicide sprays. In some areas glyphosate resistant weeds have developed, causing farmers to switch to other herbicides. Some studies also link widespread glyphosate usage to iron deficiencies in some crops, which is both a crop production and a nutritional quality concern, with potential economic and health implications.

Insect-resistant GMO Crops

Other GMO crops utilized by growers include insect-resistant crops, which have a gene from the soil bacterium *Bacillus thuringiensis* (Bt), which produces a toxin specific to insects. These crops protect plants from damage by insects; one such crop is Starlink. Another is cotton, which accounts for 63 per cent of US cotton acreage.

Some believe that similar or better pest-resistance traits can be acquired through traditional breeding practices, and resistance to various pests can be gained through hybridization or cross-pollination with wild species. In some cases, wild species are the primary source of resistance traits; some tomato cultivars that have gained resistance to at least nineteen diseases did so through crossing with wild populations of tomatoes.

Genetic engineers may someday develop transgenic plants which would allow for irrigation, drainage, conservation, sanitary engineering, and maintaining or increasing yields while requiring fewer fossil fuel derived inputs than conventional crops. Such developments would be particularly important in areas which are normally arid and rely upon constant irrigation, and on large scale farms. However, genetic engineering of plants has proven to be controversial. Many issues surrounding food security and environmental impacts have risen regarding GMO practices. For example, GMOs are questioned by some ecologists and economists concerned with GMO practices such as terminator seeds, which is a genetic modification that creates sterile seeds. Terminator seeds are currently under strong international opposition and face continual efforts of global bans. Another controversial issue is the patent protection given to companies that develop new types of seed using genetic engineering. Since companies have intellectual ownership of their seeds, they have the power to dictate terms and conditions of their patented product. Currently, ten seed companies control over two-thirds of the global seed sales. Vandana Shiva argues that these companies are guilty of biopiracy by patenting life and exploiting organisms for profit. Farmers using patented seed are restricted from saving seed for subsequent plantings, which forces farmers to buy new seed every year. Since seed saving is a traditional practice for many farmers in both developing and developed countries, GMO seeds legally bind farmers to change their seed saving practices to buying new seed every year.

Locally adapted seeds are an essential hertitage that has the potential to be lost with current hybridized crops and GMOs. Locally adapted seeds, also called land races or crop eco-types, are important because they have adapted over time to the specific microclimates, soils, other environmental conditions, field designs, and ethnic preference indigenous to the exact area of cultivation. Introducing GMOs and hybridized commercial seed to an area brings the risk of cross-pollination with local land races. Therefore, GMOs pose a threat to the sustainability of land races and the ethnic heritage of cultures. Once seed contains transgenic material, it becomes subject to the conditions of the seed company that owns the patent of the transgenic material.

There is also concern that GMOs will cross-pollinate with wild species and permanently alter native populations' genetic integrity; there are already identified populations of wild plants with transgenic genes. GMO gene flow to related weed species is a concern, as well as cross-pollination with non-transgenic crops. Since many GMO crops are harvested for their seed, such as rapeseed, seed spillage in is problematic for volunteer plants in rotated fields, as well as seed-spillage during transportation.

Food Safety and Labelling

Food security issues also coincide with food safety and food labelling concerns. Currently a global treaty, the Biosafety Protocol, regulates the trade of GMOs. The EU currently requires all GMO foods to be labelled, whereas the US does not require transparent labelling of GMO foods. Since there are still questions regarding the safety and risks associated with GMO foods, some believe the public should have the freedom to choose and know what they are eating and require all GMO products to be labelled.

Environmental Impact

Agriculture imposes external costs upon society through pesticides, nutrient runoff, excessive water usage, and assorted other problems. A 2000 assessment of agriculture in the UK determined total external costs for 1996 of £2,343 million, or £208 per hectare. A 2005 analysis of these costs in the USA concluded that cropland imposes approximately $5 to 16 billion ($30 to $96 per hectare), while livestock production imposes $714 million. Both studies concluded that more should be done to internalize external costs, and neither included subsidies in their analysis, but noted that subsidies also influence the cost of agriculture to society. Both focussed on purely fiscal impacts. The 2000 review included reported pesticide poisonings but did not include speculative chronic effects of pesticides, and the 2004 review relied on a 1992 estimate of the total impact of pesticides.

Livestock Issues

A senior UN official and co-author of a UN report detailing this problem, Henning Steinfeld, said 'Livestock are one of the most significant contributors to today's most serious environmental problems'. Livestock production occupies 70 per cent of all land used for agriculture, or 30 per cent of the land surface of the planet. It is one of the largest sources of greenhouse gases, responsible for 18 per cent of the world's greenhouse gas emissions as measured in CO_2 equivalents. By comparison, all transportation emits 13.5 per cent of the CO_2. It produces 65 per cent of human-related nitrous oxide (which has 296 times the global warming potential of $CO_{2,}$) and 37 per cent of all human-induced methane (which is 23 times as warming as CO_2. It also generates 64 per cent of the ammonia, which contributes to acid rain and acidification of ecosystems. Livestock expansion is cited as a key factor driving deforestation, in the Amazon basin 70 per cent of previously forested area is now occupied by pastures and the remainder used for feedcrops. Through deforestation and land degradation, livestock is also driving reductions in biodiversity.

Land Transformation and Degradation

Land transformation, the use of land to yield goods and services, is the most substantial way humans alter the earth's ecosystems, and is considered the driving force in the loss of biodiversity. Estimates of the amount of land transformed by humans vary from 39-50 per cent. Land degradation, the long-term decline in ecosystem function and productivity, is estimated to be occurring on 24 per cent of land worldwide, with cropland over-represented. The UN-FAO report cites land management as the driving factor behind degradation and reports that 1.5 billion people rely upon the degrading land. Degradation can be deforestation, desertification, soil erosion, mineral depletion, or chemical degradation (acidification and salinization).

Eutrophication

Eutrophication, excessive nutrients in aquatic ecosystems resulting in algal blooms and anoxia, leads to fish kills, loss of biodiversity, and renders water unfit for drinking and other industrial uses. Excessive fertilization and manure application to cropland, as well as high livestock stocking densities cause nutrient (mainly nitrogen and phosphorus) runoff and leaching from agricultural land. These nutrients are major non-point pollutants contributing to eutrophication of aquatic ecosystems.

Pesticides

Pesticide use has increased since 1950 to 2.5 million tons annually worldwide, yet crop loss from pests has remained relatively constant. The World Health Organization estimated in 1992 that 3 million pesticide poisonings occur annually, causing 220,000 deaths. Pesticides select for pesticide resistance in the pest population, leading to a condition termed the 'pesticide treadmill' in which pest resistance warrants the development of a new pesticide. An alternative argument is that the way to 'save the environment' and prevent famine is by using pesticides and intensive high yield farming, a view exemplified by a quote heading the Center for Global Food Issues website: 'Growing more per acre leaves more land for nature'. However, critics argue that a trade-off between the environment and a need for food is not inevitable, and that pesticides simply replace good agronomic practices such as crop rotation.

Climate Change

Climate change has the potential to affect agriculture through changes in temperature, rainfall (timing and quantity), CO_2, solar radiation and the interaction of these elements. Agriculture can both mitigate or worsen global warming. Some of the increase in CO_2 in the atmosphere comes from the decomposition of organic matter in the soil, and much of the methane emitted into the atmosphere is caused by the decomposition of organic matter in wet soils such as rice paddies. Further, wet or anaerobic soils also lose nitrogen through denitrification, releasing the greenhouse gas nitric oxide. Changes in management can reduce the release of these greenhouse gases, and soil can further be used to sequester some of the CO_2 in the atmosphere.

Distortions in Modern Global Agriculture

Differences in economic development, population density and culture mean that the farmers of the world operate under very different conditions.

A US cotton farmer may receive US$230 in government subsidies per acre planted (in 2003), while farmers in Mali and other third-world countries do without. When prices decline, the heavily subsidised US farmer is not forced to reduce his output, making it difficult for cotton prices to rebound, but his Mali counterpart may go broke in the meantime.

A livestock farmer in South Korea can calculate with a (highly subsidized) sales price of US $1300 for a calf produced. A South American Mercosur country rancher calculates with a calf's sales price of US $120–200 (both 2008 figures). With the former, scarcity and high cost of land is compensated with public subsidies, the latter compensates absence of subsidies with economics of scale and low cost of land.

In the Peoples Republic of China, a rural household's productive asset may be one hectare of farmland. In Brazil, Paraguay and other countries where local legislature allows such purchases, international investors buy thousands of hectares of farmland or raw land at prices of a few hundred US $ per hectare.

Since the 1940s, agricultural productivity has increased dramatically, due largely to the increased use of energy-intensive mechanization, fertilizers and pesticides.

The vast majority of this energy input comes from fossil fuel sources. Between 1950 and 1984, the Green Revolution transformed agriculture around the globe, with world grain production increasing by 250 per cent as world population doubled. Modern agriculture's heavy reliance on petrochemicals and mechanization has raised concerns that oil shortages could increase costs and reduce agricultural output, causing food shortages.

Modern or industrialized agriculture is dependent on fossil fuels in two fundamental ways: (1) direct consumption on the farm; and (2) indirect consumption to manufacture inputs used on the farm. Direct consumption includes the use of lubricants and fuels to operate farm vehicles and machinery and use of gas, liquid propane, and electricity to power dryers, pumps, lights, heaters, and coolers. American farms directly consumed about 1.2 exajoules (1.1 quadrillion BTU) in 2002, or just over 1 per cent of the nation's total energy. Indirect consumption is mainly oil and natural gas used to manufacture fertilizers and pesticides, which accounted for 0.6 exajoules (0.6 quadrillion BTU) in 2002. The energy used to manufacture farm machinery is also a form of indirect agricultural energy consumption, but it is not included in USDA estimates of U.S. agricultural energy use. Together, direct and indirect consumption by U.S. farms accounts for about 2 per cent of the nation's energy use. Direct and indirect energy consumption by U.S. farms peaked in 1979, and has gradually declined over the past 30 years.

Food systems encompass not just agricultural production, but also off-farm processing, packaging, transporting, marketing, consumption, and disposal of food and food-related items. Agriculture accounts for approximately one-fifth of food system energy use in the United States.

Oil shortages could impact this food supply. Some farmers using modern organic-farming methods have reported yields as high as those available from conventional farming without the use of synthetic fertilizers and pesticides. However, the reconditioning of soil to restore nutrients lost during the use of monoculture agriculture techniques made possible by petroleum-based technology takes time.

In 2007, higher incentives for farmers to grow non-food biofuel crops combined with other factors (such as over-development of former farm lands, rising transportation costs, climate change, growing consumer demand in China and India, and population growth) to cause food shortages in Asia, the Middle East, Africa, and Mexico, as well as rising food prices around the globe. As of December 2007, 37 countries faced food crises, and 20 had imposed some sort of food-price controls. Some of these shortages resulted in food riots and even deadly stampedes.

The biggest fossil fuel input to agriculture is the use of natural gas as a hydrogen source for the Haber-Bosch fertilizer-creation process. Natural gas is used because it is the cheapest currently available source of hydrogen. When oil production becomes so scarce that natural gas is used as a partial stopgap replacement, and hydrogen use in transportation increases, natural gas will become much more expensive. If the Haber Process is unable to be commercialized using renewable energy (such as by electrolysis) or if other sources of hydrogen are not available to replace the Haber Process, in amounts sufficient to supply transportation and agricultural needs, this major source of fertilizer would either become extremely expensive or unavailable. This would either cause food shortages or dramatic rises in food prices.

Mitigation of Effects of Petroleum Shortages

One effect oil shortages could have on agriculture is a full return to organic agriculture. In light of peak-oil concerns, organic methods are more sustainable than contemporary practices because they use no petroleum-based pesticides, herbicides, or fertilizers. Some farmers using modern organic-farming methods have reported yields as high as those available from conventional farming. Organic farming may however be more labour-intensive and would require a shift of the workforce from urban to rural areas.

It has been suggested that rural communities might obtain fuel from the biochar and synfuel process, which uses agricultural *waste* to provide charcoal fertilizer, some fuel and food, instead of the normal food *vs* fuel debate. As the synfuel would be used on-site, the process would be more efficient and might just provide enough fuel for a new organic-agriculture fusion.

It has also been suggested that some transgenic plants may some day be developed which would allow for maintaining or increasing yields while requiring fewer fossil-fuel-derived inputs than conventional crops. The possibility of success of these programmes is questioned by ecologists and economists concerned with unsustainable GMO practices such as terminator seeds and a January 2008 report shows that GMO practices 'fail to deliver environmental, social and economic benefits'. While there has been some research on sustainability using GMO crops, at least one hyped and prominent multi-year attempt by Monsanto Company has been unsuccessful, though during the same period traditional breeding techniques yielded a more sustainable variety of the same crop. Additionally, a survey by the bio-tech industry of subsistence farmers in Africa to discover what GMO research would most benefit sustainable agriculture only identified non-transgenic issues as areas needing to be addressed. Nevertheless, some governments in Africa continue to view investments in new transgenic technologies as an essential component of efforts to improve sustainability.

4 Agronomy

Agronomy is the science and technology of using plants for food, fuel, feed, and fiber. Agronomy encompasses work in the areas of plant genetics, plant physiology, meteorology, and soil science. Agronomy is the application of a combination of sciences like biology, chemistry, ecology, earth science, and genetics. Agronomists today are involved with many issues including producing food, creating healthier food, managing environmental impact of agriculture, and creating energy from plants. Agronomists often specialize in areas such as crop rotation, irrigation and drainage, plant breeding, soil classification, soil fertility, weed control, insect and pest control.

This area of agronomy involves selective breeding of plants to produce the best crops under various conditions. Plant breeding has increased crop yields and has improved the nutritional value of numerous crops, including corn, soybeans, and wheat. It also has led to the development of new types of plants. For example, a hybrid grain called triticale was produced by crossbreeding rye and wheat. Triticale contains more usable protein than does either rye or wheat. Agronomy has also been instrumental in fruit and vegetable production research. It is understood that the role of agronomist includes seeing whether produce from a field of 'x' meets the following conditions:

- Land and water access
- Commercialization (market)
- Quality and quantity of inputs
- Risk protection (insurance)
- Agricultural credit

Biotechnology

Agronomists use biotechnology to extend and expedite the development of desired characteristics listed in the Plant Breeding section. Biotechnology is often a lab activity requiring field testing of the new crop varieties that are developed.

In addition to increasing crop yields, reducing crop vulnerability to environmental stresses, improving health and taste of foods, and reducing the need for field applied chemicals, agronomic biotechnology is increasingly being applied for novel uses other than food. For example, oilseed is at present used mainly for margarine and other food oils, but it can be modified to produce fatty acids for detergents, substitute fuels and petrochemicals.

Agronomists study sustainable ways to make soils more productive and profitable. They classify soils and reproduce them to determine whether they contain substances vital to plant growth such as compounds of nitrogen, phosphorus, and potassium. If a certain soil is deficient in these substances, fertilizers may provide them. Soil science also involves investigation of the movement of nutrients through the soil, the amount of nutrients absorbed by a plant's roots, and the development of roots and their relation to the soil.

Soil Conservation

In addition, agronomists develop methods to preserve the soil and to decrease the effects of erosion by wind and water. For example, a technique called contour plowing may be used to prevent soil erosion and conserve rainfall. Researchers in agronomy also seek ways to use the soil more effectively in solving other problems. Such problems include the disposal of human and animal wastes; water pollution; and the build-up in the soil of pesticides. No-tilling crops is a technique now used to help prevent erosion. Planting of soil binding grasses along contours can be tried in steep slopes. For better effect, contour drains of depths up to 1 metre may help retain the soil and prevent permanent wash off.

Agroecology

Agroecology is the management of agricultural systems with an emphasis on ecological and environmental perspectives. This area is closely associated with work in the areas of sustainable agriculture, organic farming, alternative food systems and the development of alternative cropping systems.

Past agricultural research has created higher yielding crops, crops with better resistance to pests and plant pathogens, and more effective fertilizers and pesticides. Research is still necessary, however, particularly as insects and diseases continue to adapt to pesticides and as soil fertility and water quality continue to need improvement.

Emerging biotechnologies will play an ever larger role in agricultural research. Scientists will be needed to apply these technologies to the creation of new food products and other advances. Moreover, increasing demand is expected for biofuels and other agricultural products used in industrial processes. Agricultural scientists will be needed to find ways to increase the output of crops used in these products.

Agronomists will also be needed to balance increased agricultural output with protection and preservation of soil, water, and ecosystems. They increasingly encourage the practice of sustainable agriculture by developing and implementing plans to manage pests, crops, soil fertility and erosion, and animal waste in ways that reduce the use of harmful chemicals and do little damage to farms and the natural environment.

Most agronomists are consultants, researchers, or teachers. Many work for agricultural experiment stations, federal or state government agencies, industrial firms, or universities. Agronomists also serve in such international organizations as the Agency for International Development, The United States Department of Agriculture, and the Food and Agriculture Organization of the United Nations.

Agronomy Schools

Agronomy programmes are offered at colleges, universities, and specialized agricultural educations. Agronomy programmes often involve classes across a range of departments including agriculture, biology, chemistry, and physiology. They can usually take from four to twelve years. Many companies will pay and agronomists in trainings way through college if they agree to work for them when they graduate.

Career Outlook

Past agricultural research has created higher yielding crops, crops with better resistance to pests and plant pathogens, and more effective fertilizers and pesticides. Research is still necessary, however, particularly as insects and diseases continue to adapt to pesticides and as soil fertility and water quality continue to need improvement.

5 Irrigation

Irrigation is an artificial application of water to the soil. It is used to assist in the growing of agricultural crops, maintenance of landscapes, and revegetation of disturbed soils in dry areas and during periods of inadequate rainfall. Additionally, irrigation also has a few other uses in crop production, which include protecting plants against frost, suppressing weed growing in grain fields and helping in preventing soil consolidation. In contrast, agriculture that relies only on direct rainfall is referred to as rain-fed or dryland farming. Irrigation systems are also used for dust suppression, disposal of sewage, and in mining. Irrigation is often studied together with drainage, which is the natural or artificial removal of surface and sub-surface water from a given area.

Irrigation is also a term used in medical/dental fields to refer to flushing and washing out anything with water or another liquid.

Archaeological investigation has identified evidence of irrigation in Mesopotamia, Egypt and Iran as far back as the 6th millennium BCE, where barley was grown in areas where the natural rainfall was insufficient to support such a crop.

In the Zana Valley of the Andes Mountains in Peru, archaeologists found remains of three irrigation canals radiocarbon dated from the 4th millennium BCE, the 3rd millennium BCE and the 9th century CE. These canals are the earliest record of irrigation in the New World. Traces of a canal possibly dating from the 5th millennium BCE were found under the 4th millennium canal. Sophisticated irrigation and storage systems were developed by the Indus Valley Civilization in Pakistan and North India, including the reservoirs at Girnar in 3000 BCE and an early canal irrigation system from circa 2600 BCE. Large scale agriculture was practiced and an extensive network of canals was used for the purpose of irrigation.

There is evidence of the ancient Egyptian pharaoh Amenemhet III in the twelfth dynasty (about 1800 BCE) using the natural lake of the Faiyum Oasis as a reservoir to store surpluses of water for use during the dry seasons, as the lake swelled annually as caused by the annual flooding of the Nile.

The Qanats, developed in ancient Persia in about 800 BCE, are among the oldest known irrigation methods still in use today. They are now found in Asia, the middle east and north Africa. The system comprises a network of vertical wells and gently sloping tunnels driven into the sides of cliffs and steep hills to tap groundwater. The noria, a water wheel with clay pots around the rim powered by the flow of the stream (or by animals where the water source was still), was first brought into use at about this time, by Roman settlers in North Africa. By 150 BCE the pots were fitted with valves to allow smoother filling as they were forced into the water.

The irrigation works of ancient Sri Lanka, the earliest dating from about 300 BCE, in the reign of King Pandukabhaya and under continuous development for the next thousand years, were one of the most complex irrigation systems of the ancient world. In addition to underground canals, the Sinhalese were the first to build completely artificial reservoirs to store water. Due to their engineering superiority in this sector, they were often called 'masters of irrigation'. Most of these irrigation systems still exist undamaged up to now, in Anuradhapura and Polonnaruwa, because of the advanced and precise engineering. The system was extensively restored and further extended during the reign of King Parakrama Bahu (1153-1186 CE).

The oldest known hydraulic engineers of China were Sunshu Ao (6th century BCE) of the Spring and Autumn Period and Ximen Bao (5th century BCE) of the Warring States period, both of whom worked on large irrigation projects. In the Szechwan region belonging to the State of Qin of ancient China, the Dujiangyan Irrigation System was built in 256 BCE to irrigate an enormous area of farmland that today still supplies water. By the 2nd century AD, during the Han Dynasty, the Chinese also used chain pumps that lifted water from lower elevation to higher elevation. These were powered by manual foot pedal, hydraulic waterwheels, or rotating mechanical wheels pulled by oxen. The water was used for public works of providing water for urban residential quarters and palace gardens, but mostly for irrigation of farmland canals and channels in the fields.

In fifteenth century Korea the world's first water gauge, *uryanggye*, was discovered in 1441 CE. The inventor was Jang Yeong-sil, a Korean engineer of the Joseon Dynasty, under the active direction of the king, Sejong the Great. It was installed in irrigation tanks as part of a nationwide system to measure and collect rainfall for agricultural applications. With this instrument, planners and farmers could make better use of the information gathered in the survey.

Present Extent

In the middle of the 20th century, the advent of diesel and electric motors led for the first time to systems that could pump groundwater out of major aquifers faster than it was recharged. This can lead to permanent loss of aquifer capacity, decreased water quality, ground subsidence, and other problems. The future of food production in such areas as the North China Plain, the Punjab, and the Great Plains of the US is threatened.

At the global scale 2,788,000 km^2 (689 million acres) of agricultural land was equipped with irrigation infrastructure around the year 2000. About 68 per cent of the area equipped for irrigation is located in Asia, 17 per cent in America, 9 per cent in Europe, 5 per cent in Africa and 1 per cent in Oceania. The largest contiguous areas of high irrigation density are found in North India and Pakistan along the rivers Ganges and Indus, in the Hai He, Huang He and Yangtze basins in China, along the Nile river in Egypt and Sudan, in the Mississippi-Missouri river basin and in parts of California. Smaller irrigation areas are spread across almost all populated parts of the world.

Types of Irrigation

Various types of irrigation techniques differ in how the water obtained from the source is distributed within the field. In general, the goal is to supply the entire field uniformly with water, so that each plant has the amount of water it needs, neither too much nor too little.

Surface Irrigation

In surface irrigation systems water moves over and across the land by simple gravity flow in order to wet it and to infiltrate into the soil. Surface irrigation can be subdivided into furrow, borderstrip or basin irrigation. It is often called flood irrigation when the irrigation results in flooding or near flooding of the cultivated land. Historically, this has been the most common method of irrigating agricultural land.

Where water levels from the irrigation source permit, the levels are controlled by dikes, usually plugged by soil. This is often seen in terraced rice fields (rice paddies), where the method is used to flood or control the level of water in each distinct field. In some cases, the water is pumped, or lifted by human or animal power to the level of the land.

Localized irrigation is a system where water is distributed under low pressure through a piped network, in a pre-determined pattern, and applied as a small discharge to each plant or adjacent to it. Drip irrigation, spray or micro-sprinkler irrigation and bubbler irrigation belong to this category of irrigation methods.

Drip irrigation, also known as trickle irrigation, functions as its name suggests. Water is delivered at or near the root zone of plants, drop by drop. This method can be the most water-efficient method of irrigation, if managed properly, since evaporation and runoff are minimized. In modern agriculture, drip irrigation is often combined with plastic mulch, further reducing evaporation, and is also the means of delivery of fertilizer. The process is known as *fertigation*.

Deep percolation, where water moves below the root zone, can occur if a drip system is operated for too long of a duration or if the delivery rate is too high. Drip irrigation methods range from very high-tech and computerized to low-tech and labor-intensive. Lower water pressures are usually needed than for most other types of systems, with the exception of low energy center pivot systems and surface irrigation systems, and the system can be designed for uniformity throughout a field or for precise water delivery to individual plants in a landscape containing a mix of plant species. Although it is difficult to regulate pressure on steep slopes, pressure compensating emitters are available, so the field does not have to be level. High-tech solutions involve precisely calibrated emitters located along lines of tubing that extend from a computerized set of valves. Both pressure regulation and filtration to remove particles are important. The tubes are usually black (or buried under soil or mulch) to prevent the growth of algae and to protect the polyethylene from degradation due to ultraviolet light. But drip irrigation can also be as low-tech as a porous clay vessel sunk into the soil and occasionally filled from a hose or bucket. Subsurface drip irrigation has been used successfully on lawns, but it is more expensive than a more traditional sprinkler system. Surface drip systems are not cost-effective (or aesthetically pleasing) for lawns and golf courses. In the past one of the main disadvantages of the subsurface drip irrigation (SDI) systems, when used for turf, was the fact of having to install the plastic lines very close to each other in the ground, therefore disrupting the turfgrass area. Recent technology developments on drip installers like the drip installer at New Mexico State University Arrow Head Center, places the line underground and covers the slit leaving no soil exposed.

Sprinkler Irrigation

In sprinkler or overhead irrigation, water is piped to one or more central locations within the field and distributed by overhead high-pressure sprinklers or guns. A system utilizing sprinklers, sprays, or guns mounted overhead on permanently installed risers is often referred to as a *solid-set* irrigation system. Higher pressure sprinklers that rotate are called *rotors* and are driven by a ball drive, gear drive, or impact mechanism. Rotors can be designed to rotate in a full or partial circle. Guns are similar to rotors, except that they generally operate at very high pressures of 40 to 130 lbf/in^2 (275 to 900 kPa) and flows of 50 to 1200 US gal/min (3 to 76 L/s), usually with nozzle diameters in the range of 0.5 to 1.9 inches (10 to 50 mm). Guns are used not only for irrigation, but also for industrial applications such as dust suppression and logging.

Sprinklers may also be mounted on moving platforms connected to the water source by a hose. Automatically moving wheeled systems known as *travelling sprinklers* may irrigate areas such as small farms, sports fields, parks, pastures, and cemeteries unattended. Most of these utilize a length of polyethylene tubing wound on a steel drum. As the tubing is wound on the drum powered by the irrigation water or a small gas engine, the sprinkler is pulled across the field. When the sprinkler arrives back at the reel the system shuts off. This type of system is known to most people as a 'waterreel' travelling irrigation sprinkler and they are used extensively for dust suppression, irrigation, and land application of waste water. Other travellers use a flat rubber hose that is dragged along behind while the sprinkler platform is pulled by a cable. These cable-type travellers are definitely old technology and their use is limited in today's modern irrigation projects.

Center Pivot Irrigation

Center pivot irrigation is a form of sprinkler irrigation consisting of several segments of pipe (usually galvanized steel or aluminum) joined together and supported by trusses, mounted on wheeled towers with sprinklers positioned along its length. The system moves in a circular pattern and is fed with water from the pivot point at the center of the arc. These systems are common in parts of the United States where terrain is flat.

Center pivot with drop sprinklers. Photo by Gene Alexander, USDA Natural Resources Conservation Service.

Most center pivot systems now have drops hanging from a u-shaped pipe called a *gooseneck* attached at the top of the pipe with sprinkler heads that are positioned a few feet (at most) above the crop, thus limiting evaporative losses. Drops can also be used with drag hoses or bubblers that deposit the water directly on the ground between crops. The crops are planted in a circle to conform to the center pivot. This type of system is known as LEPA (Low Energy Precision Application). Originally, most center pivots were water powered. These were replaced by hydraulic systems

(*T-L Irrigation*) and electric motor driven systems (*T-L, Reinke, Valley, Zimmatic*). Most sprinklers features GPS devices. Reinkes usually have strobe lights and are red. Valleys have a blue label, while Zimmatics' lights are high with either a red or white Zimmatic label.

Lateral Move (Side Roll, Wheel Line) Irrigation

A series of pipes, each with a wheel of about 1.5 m diameter permanently affixed to its midpoint and sprinklers along its length, are coupled together at one edge of a field. Water is supplied at one end using a large hose. After sufficient water has been applied, the hose is removed and the remaining assembly rotated either by hand or with a purpose-built mechanism, so that the sprinklers move 10 m across the field. The hose is reconnected. The process is repeated until the opposite edge of the field is reached. This system is less expensive to install than a center pivot, but much more labour intensive to operate, and it is limited in the amount of water it can carry. Most systems utilize 4 or 5-inch (130 mm) diameter aluminum pipe. One feature of a lateral move system is that it consists of sections that can be easily disconnected. They are most often used for small or oddly-shaped fields, such as those found in hilly or mountainous regions, or in regions where labour is inexpensive.

Sub-irrigation

Subirrigation also sometimes called *seepage irrigation* has been used for many years in field crops in areas with high water tables. It is a method of artificially raising the water table to allow the soil to be moistened from below the plants' root zone. Often those systems are located on permanent grasslands in lowlands or river valleys and combined with drainage infrastructure. A system of pumping stations, canals, weirs and gates allows it to increase or decrease the water level in a network of ditches and thereby control the water table.

Sub-irrigation is also used in commercial greenhouse production, usually for potted plants. Water is delivered from below, absorbed upwards, and the excess collected for recycling. Typically, a solution of water and nutrients floods a container or flows through a trough for a short period of time, 10–20 minutes, and is then pumped back into a holding tank for reuse. Sub-irrigation in greenhouses requires fairly sophisticated, expensive equipment and management. Advantages are water and nutrient conservation, and labor-saving through lowered system maintenance and automation. It is similar in principle and action to subsurface drip irrigation.

Manual Irrigation Using Buckets or Watering Cans

These systems have low requirements for infrastructure and technical equipment but need high labour inputs. Irrigation using watering cans is to be found for example in peri-urban agriculture around large cities in some African countries.

Automatic, Non-electric Irrigation Using Buckets and Ropes

Besides the common manual watering by bucket, an automated, natural version of this also exist. Using plain polyester ropes combined with a prepared ground mixture can be used to water plants from a vessel filled with water.

The ground mixture would need to be made depending on the plant itself, yet would mostly consist of black potting soil, vermiculite and perlite. This system would (with certain crops) allow to save expenses as it does not consume any electricity and only little water (unlike sprinklers, water timers, ...). However, it may only be used with certain crops (probably mostly larger crops that do not need a humid environment; perhaps e.g. paprikas).

Irrigation Using Stones to Catch Water from Humid Air

In countries where at night, humid air sweeps the countryside, stones are used to catch water from the humid air by condensation. This is for example practiced in the vineyards at Lanzarote.

Dry Terraces for Irrigation and Water Distribution

In subtropical countries as Mali and Senegal, a special type of terracing (without flood irrigation or intent to flatten farming ground) is used. Here, a 'stairs' is made through the use of ground level differences which helps to decrease water evaporation and also distributes the water to all patches (sort of irrigation).

Sources of Irrigation Water

Sources of irrigation water can be groundwater extracted from springs or by using wells, surface water withdrawn from rivers, lakes or reservoirs or non-conventional sources like treated wastewater, desalinated water or drainage water. A special form of irrigation using surface water is spate irrigation, also called floodwater harvesting. In case of a flood (spate) water is diverted to normally dry river beds (wadi's) using a network of dams, gates and channels and spread over large areas. The moisture stored in the soil will be used thereafter to grow crops. Spate irrigation areas are in particular located in semi-arid or arid, mountainous regions. While floodwater harvesting belongs to the accepted irrigation methods, rainwater harvesting is usually not considered as a form of irrigation. Rainwater harvesting is the collection of runoff water from roofs or unused land and the concentration of this.

How an In-ground Irrigation System Works

Most commercial and residential irrigation systems are 'in-ground' systems, which means that everything is buried in the ground. With the pipes, sprinklers, and irrigation valves being hidden, it makes for a cleaner, more presentable landscape without garden hoses or other items having to be moved around manually. This does, however, create some drawbacks in the maintenance of a completely buried system.

Water Source and Piping

The beginning of a sprinkler system is the water source. This is usually a tap into an existing (city) water line or a pump that pulls water out of a well or a pond. The water travels through pipes from the water source through the valves to the sprinklers. The pipes from the water source up to the irrigation valves are called 'mainlines', and the lines from the valves to the sprinklers are called 'lateral lines'. Most piping used in irrigation systems today are HDPE and MDPE or PVC or PEX plastic pressure pipes due to their ease of installation and resistance to corrosion. After the water source, the water usually travels through a check valve. This prevents water in the irrigation lines from being pulled back into and contaminating the clean water supply.

Controllers, Zones, and Valves

Most Irrigation systems are divided into zones. A zone is a single Irrigation Valve and one or a group of sprinklers that are connected by pipes. Irrigation Systems are divided into zones because there is usually not enough pressure and available flow to run sprinklers for an entire yard or sports field at once. Each zone has a solenoid valve on it that is controlled via wire by an Irrigation Controller. The Irrigation Controller is either a mechanical or electrical device that signals a zone to turn on at a specific time and keeps it on for a specified amount of time. 'Smart Controller' is a recent term used to describe a controller that is capable of adjusting the watering time by itself in response to current environmental conditions. The smart controller determines current conditions by means of historic weather data for the local area, a soil moisture sensors (water potential or water content), weather station, or a combination of these.

Sprinklers

When a zone comes on, the water flows through the lateral lines and ultimately ends up at the irrigation

Sprinkler heads. Most sprinklers have pipe thread inlets on the bottom of them which allows a fitting and the pipe to be attached to them. The sprinklers are usually installed with the top of the head flush with the ground surface. When the water is pressurized, the head will pop up out of the ground and water the desired area until the valve closes and shuts off that zone. Once there is no more water pressure in the lateral line, the sprinkler head will retract back into the ground.

Problems in Irrigation

- Competition for surface water rights.
- Depletion of underground quifers.
- Ground subsidence (e.g. New Orleans, Louisiana)

Under-irrigation or irrigation giving only just enough water for the plant (e.g. in drip line irrigation) gives poor soil salinity control which leads to increased soil salinity with consequent build up of toxic salts on soil surface in areas with high evaporation. This requires either leaching to remove these salts and a method of drainage to carry the salts away. When using drip lines, the leaching is best done regularly at certain intervals (with only a slight excess of water), so that the salt is flushed back under the plant's roots.

Over-irrigation because of poor distribution uniformity or management wastes water, chemicals, and may lead to water pollution. Deep drainage (from over-irrigation) may result in rising water tables which in some instances will lead to problems of irrigation salinity. Irrigation with saline or high-sodium water may damage soil structure.

6 Fertilizer

Fertilizers are soil amendments applied to promote plant growth; the main nutrients present in fertilizer are nitrogen, phosphorus, and potassium (the 'macronutrients') and other nutrients ('micronutrients') are added in smaller amounts. Fertilizers are usually directly applied to soil, and also sprayed on leaves ('foliar feeding').

Fertilizers are roughly broken up between *organic* and *inorganic* fertilizer, with the main difference between the two being sourcing, and not necessarily differences in nutrient content.

Organic fertilizers and some mined inorganic fertilizers have been used for many centuries, whereas chemically-synthesized inorganic fertilizers were only widely developed during the industrial revolution. Increased understanding and use of fertilizers were important parts of the pre-industrial British Agricultural Revolution and the industrial green revolution of the 20th century.

Plant Nutrients Supplied by Fertilizers

Tennessee Valley Authority: 'Results of Fertilizer' demonstration 1942.

Fertilizers typically provide, in varying proportions:

- the three primary macronutrients: nitrogen, phosphorus, and potassium.
- the three secondary macronutrients such as calcium (Ca), sulfur (S), magnesium (Mg); and
- the micronutrients or trace minerals: boron (Bo), chlorine (Cl), manganese (Mn), iron (Fe), zinc (Zn), copper (Cu), molybdenum (Mo) and selenium (Se).

The macronutrients are consumed in larger quantities and are present in plant tissue in quantities from 0.2 per cent to 4.0 per cent (on a dry matter weight basis). Micronutrients are consumed in smaller quantities and are present in plant tissue in quantities measured in parts per million (ppm), ranging from 5 to 200 ppm, or less than 0.02 per cent dry weight.

LABELLING OF FERTILIZERS

Macronutrient Fertilizers

Macronutrient fertilizers are labelled with an *NPK* analysis and a, 'N-P-K-S' in Australia.

An example of labelling for the fertilizer *potash* is composed of 1:1 potassium to chloride or 52 per cent potassium and 48 per cent chlorine *by weight* (owing to differences in molecular weight between the elements). Traditional analysis of 100g of *KCl* would yield 60g of K_2O. The *percentage yield* of K_2O from the original 100g of fertilizer is the number shown on the label. A potash fertilizer would thus be labelled 0-0-60, *not* 0-0-52.

History

The modern understanding of plant nutrition dates to the 19th century and the work of Justus von Liebig, among others. Management of soil fertility, however, has been the pre-occupation of farmers for thousands of years.

Inorganic Fertilizer (Synthetic Fertilizer)

Fertilizers are broadly divided into *organic fertilizers* (composed of enriched organic matter—plant or animal), or *inorganic fertilizers* (composed of synthetic chemicals and/ or minerals).

Inorganic fertilizer is often synthesized using the Haber-Bosch process, which produces ammonia as the end product. This ammonia is used as a feedstock for other nitrogen fertilizers, such as anhydrous ammonium nitrate and urea. These concentrated products may be diluted with water to form a concentrated liquid fertilizer (e.g. UAN). Ammonia can be combined with rock phosphate and potassium fertilizer in the Odda Process to produce *compound fertilizer*.

The use of synthetic nitrogen fertilisers has increased steadily in the last 50 years, rising almost 20-fold to the current rate of 1 billion tonnes of nitrogen per year. The use of phosphate fertilisers has also increased from 9 million tonnes per year in 1960 to 40 million tonnes per year in 2000. A maize crop yielding 6-9 tonnes of grain per hectare requires 30-50 kg of phosphate fertiliser to be applied, soybean requires 20-25 kg per hectare. Yara International is the world's largest producer of nitrogen based fertilisers.

Synthetic fertilizers are commonly used to treat fields used for growing maize, followed by barley, sorghum, rapeseed, soy and sunflower. One study has shown that application of nitrogen fertilizer on off-season cover crops can increase the biomass (and subsequent green manure value) of these crops, while having a beneficial effect on soil nitrogen levels for the main crop planted during the summer season.

PROBLEMS OF INORGANIC FERTILIZER

Trace Mineral Depletion

Many inorganic fertilizers do not replace trace mineral elements in the soil which become gradually depleted by crops. This depletion has been linked to studies which have shown a marked fall (up to 75 per cent) in the quantities of such minerals present in fruit and vegetables.

However, a recent review of 55 scientific studies concluded "there is no evidence of a difference in nutrient quality between organically and conventionally produced foodstuffs". Conversely, a major long-term study funded by the European Union found that organically-produced milk and produce were significantly higher in antioxidants (such as carotenoids and alpha-linoleic acids) than their conventionally grown counterparts.

In Western Australia deficiencies of zinc, copper, manganese, iron and molybdenum were identified as limiting the growth of broad-acre crops and pastures in the 1940s and 1950s . Soils in Western Australia are very old, highly weathered and deficient in many of the major nutrients and trace elements . Since this time these trace elements are routinely added to inorganic fertilizers used in agriculture in this state.

Over-fertilization of a vital nutrient can be as detrimental as underfertilization. 'Fertilizer burn' can occur when too much fertilizer is applied, resulting in a drying out of the roots and damage or even death of the plant.

High Energy Consumption

The production of *synthetic* ammonia currently consumes about 5 per cent of global natural gas consumption, which is somewhat under two per cent of world energy production.

Natural gas is overwhelmingly used for the production of ammonia, but other energy sources, together with a hydrogen source, can be used for the production of nitrogen compounds suitable for fertilizers. The cost of natural gas makes up about 90 per cent of the cost of producing ammonia. The increase in price of natural gases over the past decade, along with other factors such as increasing demand, have contributed to an increase in fertilizer price.

Long-term Sustainability

Inorganic fertilizers are now produced in ways which cannot be continued indefinitely. Potassium and phosphorus come from mines (or saline lakes such as the Dead Sea) and such resources are limited. Atmospheric (*unfixed*) nitrogen is effectively unlimited (forming over 70 per cent of the atmospheric gases), but this is not in a form useful to plants. To make nitrogen accessible to plants requires nitrogen fixation (conversion of atmospheric nitrogen to a plant-accessible form).

Artificial nitrogen fertilizers are typically synthesized using fossil fuels such as natural gas and coal, which are limited resources. In lieu of converting natural gas to syngas for use in the Haber process, it is also possible to convert renewable biomass to syngas (or wood gas) to supply the necessary energy for the process, though the amount of land and resources (ironically often including fertilzer) necessary for such a project may be prohibitive.

Benefits of Organic Fertilizer

In addition to increasing yield and fertilizing plants directly, organic fertilizers can improve the biodiversity (soil life) and long-term productivity of soil , and may prove a large depository for excess carbon dioxide.

Organic nutrients increase the abundance of soil organisms by providing organic matter and micronutrients for organisms such as fungal mycorrhiza, (which aid plants in absorbing nutrients), and can drastically reduce external inputs of pesticides, energy and fertilizer, at the cost of decreased yield.

Comparison with Inorganic Fertilizer

Organic fertilizer nutrient content, solubility, and nutrient release rates are typically all lower than inorganic fertilizers. One study found that over a 140-day period, after seven leachings:

- Organic fertilizers had released between 25 per cent and 60 per cent of their nitrogen content.
- Controlled release fertilizers (CRFs) had a relatively constant rate of release.
- Soluble fertilizer released most of its nitrogen content at the first leaching.

In general, the nutrients in organic fertilizer are both more dilute and also much less readily available to plants. According to UC IPM, all *organic fertilizers* are classified as 'slow-release' fertilizers, and therefore cannot cause nitrogen burn.

Animal-sourced Urea, are suitable for application organic agriculture, while pure synthetic forms of urea are not. The common thread that can be seen through these examples is that *organic* agriculture attempts to define itself through minimal processing (in contrast to the man-made Haber process), as well as being naturally-occurring or via natural biological processes such as composting.

Sewage sludge use in organic agricultural operations in the U.S. has been extremely limited and rare due to USDA prohibition of the practice (due to toxic metal accumulation, among other factors). The USDA now requires 3rd-party certification of high-nitrogen liquid organic fertilizers sold in the U.S.

Plant

Cover crops are also grown to enrich soil as a green manure through nitrogen fixation from the atmosphere; as well as phosphorus (through nutrient mobilization) content of soils.

Mineral

Naturally mined powdered limestone, mined rock phosphate and sodium nitrate, are *inorganic* (in a *chemical* sense), are energetically-intensive to harvest, yet are approved for usage in organic agriculture in *minimal* amounts.

The nitrogen-rich compounds found in fertilizer run-off is the primary cause of a serious depletion of oxygen in many parts of the ocean, especially in coastal zones; the resulting lack of dissolved oxygen is greatly reducing the ability of these areas to sustain oceanic fauna. Visually, water may become cloudy and discoloured (green, yellow, brown, or red).

About half of all the lakes in the United States are now eutrophic, while the number of oceanic dead zones near inhabited coastlines are increasing. As of 2006, the application of nitrogen fertilizer is being increasingly controlled in Britain and the United States . If eutrophication *can* be reversed, it may take decades before the accumulated nitrates in groundwater can be broken down by natural processes.

High application rates of inorganic nitrogen fertilizers in order to maximize crop yields, combined with the high solubilities of these fertilizers leads to increased runoff into surface water as well as leaching into groundwater. The use of ammonium nitrate in *inorganic* fertilizers is particularly damaging, as plants absorb ammonium ions preferentially over nitrate ions, while excess nitrate ions which are not absorbed dissolve (by rain or irrigation) into runoff or groundwater.

Blue Baby Syndrome

Nitrate levels above 10 mg/L (10 ppm) in groundwater can cause 'blue baby syndrome' (acquired methemoglobinemia), leading to hypoxia (which can lead to coma and death if not treated).

The concentration of up to 100 mg/kg of cadmium in phosphate minerals (for example, minerals from Nauru and the Christmas islands increases the contamination of soil with cadmium, for example in New Zealand.

Uranium is another example of a contaminant often found in phosphate fertilizers (at levels from 7 to 100 pCi/g).

Eventually these heavy metals can build up to unacceptable levels and build up in vegetable produce. Average annual intake of uranium by adults is estimated to be about 0.5 mg (500 μg) from ingestion of food and water and 0.6 μg from breathing air.

Steel industry wastes, recycled into fertilizers for their high levels of zinc (essential to plant growth), wastes can include the following toxic metals: lead arsenic, cadmium, chromium, and nickel. The most common toxic elements in this type of fertilizer are mercury, lead, and arsenic. Concerns have been raised concerning fish meal mercury content by at least one source in Spain.

Also, highly-radioactive Polonium-210 contained in phosphate fertilizers is absorbed by the roots of plants and stored in its tissues; tobacco derived from plants fertilized by rock phosphates contains Polonium-210 which emits alpha radiation estimated to cause about 11,700 lung cancer deaths each year worldwide.

For these reasons, it is recommended that nutrient budgeting, through careful observation and monitoring of crops, take place to mitigate the effects of excess fertilizer application.

Methane emissions from crop fields (notably rice paddy fields) are increased by the application of ammonium-based fertilizers; these emissions contribute greatly to global climate change as methane is a potent greenhouse gas.

Through the increasing use of nitrogen fertilizer, which is added at a rate of 1 billion tons per year presently to the already existing amount of reactive nitrogen, nitrous oxide (N_2O) has become the third most important greenhouse gas after carbon dioxide and methane. It has a global warming potential 296 times larger than an equal mass of carbon dioxide and it also contributes to stratospheric ozone depletion.

Storage and application of some nitrogen fertilizers in some weather or soil conditions can cause emissions of the potent greenhouse gas–nitrous oxide. Ammonia gas (NH_3) may be emitted following application of 'inorganic' fertilizers and/or manures and slurries.

The use of fertilizers on a global scale emits significant quantities of greenhouse gas into the atmosphere. Emissions come about through the use of animal manures and urea, which release ethane, nitrous oxide, ammonia, and carbon dioxide in varying quantities depending on their form (solid or liquid) and management (collection, storage, fertilizers that use nitric acid or ammonium bicarbonate, the production and application of which results in emissions of nitrogen oxides, nitrous oxide, ammonia and carbon dioxide into the atmosphere.

By changing processes and procedures, it is possible to mitigate some, but not all, of these effects on anthropogenic climate change.

7 Industrial Agriculture

Industrial agriculture is a form of modern farming that refers to the industrialized production of livestock, poultry, fish, and crops. The methods of industrial agriculture are technoscientific, economic, and political. They include innovation in agricultural machinery and farming methods, genetic technology, techniques for achieving economies of scale in production, the creation of new markets for consumption, the application of patent protection to genetic information, and global trade. These methods are widespread in developed nations and increasingly prevalent worldwide. Most of the meat, dairy, eggs, fruits, and vegetables available in supermarkets are produced using these methods of industrial agriculture.

The birth of industrial agriculture more or less coincides with that of the Industrial Revolution in general. The identification of nitrogen, potassium, and phosphorus (referred to by the acronym NPK) as critical factors in plant growth led to the manufacture of synthetic fertilizers, making possible more intensive types of agriculture. The discovery of vitamins and their role in animal nutrition, in the first two decades of the 20th century, led to vitamin supplements, which in the 1920s allowed certain livestock to be raised indoors, reducing their exposure to adverse natural elements. The discovery of antibiotics and vaccines facilitated raising livestock in concentrated, controlled animal feed operations by reducing diseases caused by crowding. Chemicals developed for use in World War II gave rise to synthetic pesticides. Developments in shipping networks and technology have made long-distance distribution of agricultural produce feasible.

Agricultural production across the world doubled four times between 1820 and 1975 to feed a global population of one billion human beings in 1800 and 6.5 billion in 2002. During the same period, the number of people involved in farming dropped as the process became more automated. In the 1930s, 24 per cent of the American population worked in agriculture compared to 1.5 per cent in 2002; in 1940, each farm worker supplied 11 consumers, whereas in 2002, each worker supplied 90 consumers. The number of farms has also decreased, and their ownership is more concentrated. In the U.S., four companies kill 81 per cent of cows, 73 per cent of sheep, 57 per cent of pigs, and produce 50 per cent of chickens, cited as an example of 'vertical integration' by the president of the U.S. National Farmers' Union. In 1967, there were one million pig farms in America; as of 2002, there were 114,000, with 80 million pigs (out of 95 million) killed each year on factory farms, according to the U.S. National Pork Producers Council. According to the Worldwatch Institute, 74 per cent of the world's poultry, 43 per cent of beef, and 68 per cent of eggs are produced this way.

According to Denis Avery of the agribusiness funded Hudson Institute, Asia increased its consumption of pork by 18 million tons in the 1990s. As of 1997, the world had a stock of 900 million pigs, which Avery predicts will rise to 2.5 billion pigs by 2050. He told the College of Natural Resources at the University of California, Berkeley that three billion pigs will thereafter be needed annually to meet demand. He writes: "For the sake of the environment, we had better hope those hogs are raised in big, efficient confinement systems."

British Agricultural Revolution

The British agricultural revolution describes a period of agricultural development in Britain between the 16th century and the mid-19th century, which saw a massive increase in agricultural productivity and net output. This in turn supported unprecedented population growth, freeing up a significant percentage of the workforce, and thereby helped drive the Industrial Revolution. How this came about is not entirely clear. In recent decades, historians cited four key changes in agricultural practices, enclosure, mechanization, four-field crop rotation, and selective breeding, and gave credit to a relatively few individuals.

Challenges and Issues

The challenges and issues of industrial agriculture for global and local society, for the industrial agriculture industry, for the individual industrial agriculture farm, and for animal rights include the costs and benefits of both current practices and proposed changes to those practices. Current industrial agriculture practices are temporarily increasing the carrying capacity of the Earth for humans while slowly destroying the *long term* carrying capacity of the earth for humans necessitating a shift to a sustainable agriculture form of industrial agriculture. This is a continuation of thousands of years of the invention and use of technologies in feeding ever growing populations.

[W]hen hunter-gatherers with growing populations depleted the stocks of game and wild foods across the Near East, they were forced to introduce agriculture. But agriculture brought much longer hours of work and a less rich diet than hunter-gatherers enjoyed. Further population growth among shifting slash-and-burn farmers led to shorter fallow periods, falling yields and soil erosion. Plowing and fertilizers were introduced to deal with these problems — but once again involved longer hours of work and degradation of soil resources(Boserup, The Conditions of Agricultural Growth, Allen and Unwin, 1965, expanded and updated in Population and Technology, Blackwell, 1980).

While the point of industrial agriculture is lower cost products to create greater productivity thus a higher standard of living as measured by available goods and services, industrial methods have side effects both good and bad. Further, industrial agriculture is not some single indivisible thing, but instead is composed of numerous separate elements, each of which can be modified, and in fact is modified in response to market conditions, government regulation, and scientific advances. So the question then becomes for each specific element that goes into an industrial agriculture method or technique or process: What bad side effects are bad enough that the financial gain and good side effects are outweighed? Different interest groups not only reach different conclusions on this, but also recommend differing solutions, which then become factors in changing both market conditions and government regulations.

Society

The major challenges and issues faced by society concerning industrial agriculture include:

- Maximizing the benefits
- Cheap and plentiful food
- Convenience for the consumer

The contribution to our economy on many levels, from growers to harvesters to processors to sellers while minimizing the downsides:

- Environmental and social costs
- Damage to fisheries

- Clean-up of surface and groundwater polluted with animal waste
- Increased health risks from pesticides
- Increased ozone pollution and global warming from heavy use of fossil fuels.

Industrial agriculture treats farmed products in terms of minimizing inputs and maximizing outputs at every stage from the natural resources of sun, land and water to the consumer which results in a vertically integrated industry that genetically manipulates crops and livestock; and processes, packages, and markets in whatever way generates maximum return on investment creating convenience foods many customers will pay a premium for. A consumer backlash against food sold for taste, convenience, and profit rather than nutrition and other values (e.g. reduce waste, be natural, be ethical) has led the industry to also provide organic food, minimally processed foods, and minimally packaged foods to maximally satisfy all segments of society thus generating maximum return on investment.

LIABILITIES

Environment

Industrial agriculture uses huge amounts of water, energy, and industrial chemicals; increasing pollution in the arable land, useable water and atmosphere. Herbicides, insecticides, fertilizers, and animal waste products are accumulating in ground and surface waters. "Many of the negative effects of industrial agriculture are remote from fields and farms. Nitrogen compounds from the Midwest, for example, travel down the Mississippi to degrade coastal fisheries in the Gulf of Mexico. But other adverse effects are showing up within agricultural production systems–for example, the rapidly developing resistance among pests is rendering our arsenal of herbicides and insecticides increasingly ineffective."

Social

A study done for the US. Office of Technology Assessment conducted by the UC Davis Macrosocial Accounting Project concluded that industrial agriculture is associated with substantial deterioration of human living conditions in nearby rural communities. In addition, children living near farming areas are at higher risk of developing autism than the general population. Due to the increase of airborne pollutants and important factors. Researchers examined the residents who had autism and look at how far they lived from a landfill, concluding that the area of highest ASD (autism spectrum disorders) cases coincides with the highest density of toxic landfill sites while the area with lowest ASD cases has the lowest density of toxic landfill sites.

Animals

'Confined animal feeding operations' or 'intensive livestock operations' or 'factory farms', can hold large numbers (some up to hundreds of thousands) of animals, often indoors. These animals are typically cows, hogs, turkeys, or chickens. The distinctive characteristics of such farms is the concentration of livestock in a given space. The aim of the operation is to produce as much meat, eggs, or milk at the lowest possible cost.

Food and water is supplied in place, and artificial methods are often employed to maintain animal health and improve production, such as therapeutic use of antimicrobial agents, vitamin supplements and growth hormones. Growth hormones are not used in chicken meat production nor are they used in the European Union for any animal. In meat production, methods are also sometimes employed to control undesirable behaviours often related to stresses of being confined in restricted areas with other animals. More docile breeds are sought (with natural dominant behaviours bred out for example), physical restraints to stop interaction, such as individual cages for chickens, or animals physically modified, such as the de-beaking of chickens to reduce the harm of fighting. Weight gain is encouraged by the provision of plentiful supplies of food to animals breed for weight gain.

The designation 'confined animal feeding operation' in the U.S. resulted from that country's 1972 Federal Clean Water Act, which was enacted to protect and restore lakes and rivers to a "fishable, swimmable" quality. The United States Environmental Protection Agency (EPA) identified certain animal feeding operations, along with many other types of industry, as point source polluters of groundwater. These operations were designated as CAFOs and subject to special anti-pollution regulation.

In 24 states in the U.S., isolated cases of groundwater contamination has been linked to CAFOs. For example, the ten million hogs in North Carolina generate 19 million tons of waste per year. The U.S. federal government acknowledges the waste disposal issue and requires that animal waste be stored in lagoons. These lagoons can be as large as 7.5 acres (30,000 m^2). Lagoons not protected with an impermeable liner can leak waste into groundwater under some conditions, as can runoff from manure spread back onto fields as fertilizer in the case of an unforeseen heavy rainfall. A lagoon that burst in 1995 released 25 million gallons of nitrous sludge in North Carolina's New River. The spill allegedly killed eight to ten million fish.

The large concentration of animals, animal waste, and dead animals in a small space poses ethical issues. Animal rights and animal welfare activists have charged that intensive animal rearing is cruel to animals. As they become more common, so do concerns about air pollution and ground water contamination, and the effects on human health of the pollution and the use of antibiotics and growth hormones.

One particular problem with farms on which animals are intensively reared is the growth of antibiotic resistant bacteria. Because large numbers of animals are confined in a small space, any disease would spread quickly, and so antibiotics are used preventively. A small percentage of bacteria are not killed by the drugs, which may infect human beings if it becomes airborne.

According to the U.S. Centers for Disease Control and Prevention (CDC), farms on which animals are intensively reared can cause adverse health reactions in farm workers. Workers may develop acute and chronic lung disease, musculoskeletal injuries, and may catch infections that transmit from animals to human beings.

The CDC writes that chemical, bacterial, and viral compounds from animal waste may travel in the soil and water. Residents near such farms report nuisances such as unpleasant smells and flies, as well as adverse health effects.

The CDC has identified a number of pollutants associated with the discharge of animal waste into rivers and lakes, and into the air. The use of antibiotics may create antibiotic-resistant pathogens; parasites, bacteria, and viruses may be spread; ammonia, nitrogen, and phosphorus can reduce oxygen in surface waters and contaminate drinking water; pesticides and hormones may cause hormone-related changes in fish; animal feed and feathers may stunt the growth of desirable plants in surface waters and provide nutrients to disease-causing micro-organisms; trace elements such as arsenic and copper, which are harmful to human health, may contaminate surface waters.

Crops

The projects within the Green Revolution spread technologies that had already existed, but had not been widely used outside of industrialized nations. These technologies included pesticides, irrigation projects, and synthetic nitrogen fertilizer.

The novel technological development of the Green Revolution was the production of what some referred to as 'miracle seeds'. Scientists created strains of maize, wheat, and rice that are generally referred to as HYVs or 'high-yielding varieties'. HYVs have an increased nitrogen-absorbing potential compared to other varieties. Since cereals that absorbed extra nitrogen would typically lodge, or fall over before harvest, semi-dwarfing genes were bred into their genomes. Norin 10 wheat, a variety developed by Orville Vogel from Japanese dwarf wheat varieties, was instrumental in developing Green Revolution wheat cultivars. IR8, the first widely implemented HYV rice to be developed by the International Rice Research Institute, was created through a cross between an Indonesian variety named 'Peta' and a Chinese variety named 'Dee Geo Woo Gen'.

With the availability of molecular genetics in Arabidopsis and rice the mutant genes responsible (*reduced height(rht), gibberellin insensitive (gai1)* and *slender rice (slr1)*) have been cloned and identified as cellular signalling components of gibberellic acid, a phytohormone involved in regulating stem growth via its effect on cell division. Stem growth in the mutant background is significantly reduced leading to the dwarf phenotype. Photosynthetic investment in the stem is reduced dramatically as the shorter plants are inherently more stable mechanically. Assimilates become redirected to grain production, amplifying in particular the effect of chemical fertilisers on commercial yield.

HYVs significantly outperform traditional varieties in the presence of adequate irrigation, pesticides, and fertilizers. In the absence of these inputs, traditional varieties may outperform HYVs. One criticism of HYVs is that they were developed as F1 hybrids, meaning they need to be purchased by a farmer every season rather than saved from previous seasons, thus increasing a farmer's cost of production.

Sustainable Agriculture

The idea and practice of sustainable agriculture has arisen in response to the problems of industrial agriculture. Sustainable agriculture integrates three main goals: environmental stewardship, farm profitability, and prosperous farming communities. These goals have been defined by a variety of disciplines and may be looked at from the vantage point of the farmer or the consumer.

Organic Farming Methods

Organic farming methods combine some aspects of scientific knowledge and highly limited modern technology with traditional farming practices; accepting some of the methods of industrial agriculture while rejecting others. Organic methods rely on naturally occurring biological processes, which often take place over extended periods of time, and a holistic approach; while chemical-based farming focuses on immediate, isolated effects and reductionist strategies.

Integrated Multi-Trophic Aquaculture is an example of this holistic approach. Integrated Multi-Trophic Aquaculture (IMTA) is a practice in which the by-products (wastes) from one species are recycled to become inputs (fertilizers, food) for another. Fed aquaculture (e.g. fish, shrimp) is combined with inorganic extractive (e.g. seaweed) and organic extractive (e.g. shellfish) aquaculture to create balanced systems for environmental sustainability (biomitigation), economic stability (product diversification and risk reduction) and social acceptability (better management practices).

8 Soil

Soil is a natural body consisting of layers (soil horizons) of mineral constituents of variable thicknesses, which differ from the parent materials in their morphological, physical, chemical, and mineralogical characteristics.

It is composed of particles of broken rock that have been altered by chemical and environmental processes that include weathering and erosion. Soil differs from its parent rock due to interactions between the lithosphere, hydrosphere, atmosphere, and the biosphere.

It supports a complex ecosystem, which supports the plants on the surface and creates new soil by breaking down rocks and sand. This microscopic ecosystem has co-evolved with the plants to collect and store water and nutrients in a form usable by plants.

Soil particles pack loosely, forming a soil structure filled with pore spaces. These pores contain soil solution (liquid) and air (gas). Accordingly, soils are often treated as a three state-system. Most soils have a density between 1 and 2 g/cm^3. Soil is also known as earth: it is the substance from which our planet takes its name. Little of the soil composition of planet Earth is older than the Tertiary and most no older than the Pleistocene. In engineering, soil is referred to as regolith, or loose rock material.

Soil Forming Factors

Soil formation, or pedogenesis, is the combined effect of physical, chemical, biological, and anthropogenic processes on soil parent material. Soil genesis involves processes that develop layers or horizons in the soil profile. These processes involve additions, losses, transformations and translocations of material that compose the soil. Minerals derived from weathered rocks undergo changes that cause the formation of secondary minerals and other compounds that are variably soluble in water, these constituents are moved (translocated) from one area of the soil to other areas by water and animal activity. The alteration and movement of materials within soil causes the formation of distinctive soil horizons.

The weathering of bedrock produces the parent material from which soils form. An example of soil development from bare rock occurs on recent lava flows in warm regions under heavy and very frequent rainfall. In such climates, plants become established very quickly on basaltic lava, even though there is very little organic material. The plants are supported by the porous rock as it is filled with nutrient-bearing water which carries, for example, dissolved minerals and guano. The developing plant roots, themselves or associated with mycorrhizal fungi, gradually break up the porous lava and organic matter soon accumulates.

But even before it does, the predominantly porous broken lava in which the plant roots grow can be considered a soil. How the soil 'life' cycle proceeds is influenced by at least five classic soil forming factors that are dynamically intertwined in shaping the way soil is developed, they include: parent material, regional climate, topography, biotic potential and the passage of time.

Parent Material

The material from which soils form is called parent material. It includes: weathered primary bedrock; secondary material transported from other locations, e.g. colluvium and alluvium; deposits that are already present but mixed or altered in other ways — old soil formations, organic material including peat or alpine humus; and anthropogenic materials, like landfill or mine waste Few soils form directly from the breakdown of the underlying rocks they develop on. These soils are often called 'residual soils', and have the same general chemistry as their parent rocks. Most soils derive from materials that have been transported from other locations by wind, water and gravity. Some of these materials may have moved many miles or only a few feet. Windblown material called loess is common in the Midwest of North America and in Central Asia and other locations. Glacial till is a component of many soils in the northern and southern latitudes and those formed near large mountains; till is the product of glacial ice moving over the ground. The ice can break rock and larger stones into smaller pieces, it also can sort material into different sizes. As glacial ice melts, the melt water also moves and sorts material, and deposits it varying distances from its origin. The deeper sections of the soil profile may have materials that are relatively unchanged from when they were deposited by water, ice or wind.

Weather is the first stage in the transforming of parent material into soil material. In soils forming from bedrock, a thick layer of weathered material called saprolite may form. Saprolite is the result of weathering processes that include: hydrolysis (the replacement of a mineral's cations with hydrogen ions), chelation from organic compounds, hydration (the absorption of water by minerals), solution of minerals by water, and physical processes that include freezing and thawing or wetting and drying. The mineralogical and chemical composition of the primary bedrock material, plus physical features, including grain size and degree of consolidation, plus the rate and type of weathering, transforms it into different soil materials.

Climate

Soil formation greatly depends on the climate, and soils from different climate zones show distinctive characteristics. Temperature and moisture affect weathering and leaching. Wind moves sand and other particles, especially in arid regions where there is little plant cover. The type and amount of precipitation influence soil formation by affecting the movement of ions and particles through the soil, aiding in the development of different soil profiles. Seasonal and daily temperature fluctuations affect the effectiveness of water in weathering parent rock material and affect soil dynamics. The cycle of freezing and thawing is an effective mechanism to break up rocks and other consolidated materials. Temperature and precipitation rates affect biological activity, rates of chemical reactions and types of vegetation cover.

Biological Factors

Plants, animals, fungi, bacteria and humans affect soil formation. Animals and micro-organisms mix soils to form burrows and pores allowing moisture and gases to seep into deeper layers. In the same way, plant roots open channels in the soils, especially plants with deep taproots which can penetrate many meters through the different soil layers to bring up nutrients from deeper in the soil. Plants with fibrous roots that spread out near the soil surface, have roots that are easily decomposed, adding organic matter. Micro-organisms, including fungi and bacteria, affect chemical exchanges between roots and soil and act as a reserve of nutrients. Humans can impact soil formation by removing vegetation cover; this removal promotes erosion. They can also mix the different soil layers, restarting the soil formation process as less-weathered material is mixed with and diluting the more developed upper layers.

Vegetation impacts soils in numerous ways. It can prevent erosion from rain or surface runoff. It shades soils, keeping them cooler and slowing evaporation of soil moisture, or it can cause soils to dry out by transpiration. Plants can form new chemicals that break down or build up soil particles. Vegetation depends on climate, land form topography and biological factors. Soil factors such as soil density, depth, chemistry, pH, temperature and moisture greatly affect the type of plants that can grow in a given location. Dead plants, dropped leaves and stems of plants fall to the surface of the soil and decompose. There, organisms feed on them and mix the organic material with the upper soil layers; these organic compounds become part of the soil formation process, ultimately shaping the type of soil formed.

Time

Time is a factor in the interactions of all the above factors as they develop soil. Over time, soils evolve features dependent on the other forming factors, and soil formation is a time-responsive process dependent on how the other factors interplay with each other. Soil is always changing. For example, recently-deposited material from a flood exhibits no soil development because there has not been enough time for soil-forming activities. The soil surface is buried, and the formation process begins again for this soil. The long periods over which change occurs and its multiple influences mean that simple soils are rare, resulting in the formation of soil horizons. While soil can achieve relative stability in properties for extended periods, the soil life cycle ultimately ends in soil conditions that leave it vulnerable to erosion. Despite the inevitability of soil retrogression and degradation, most soil cycles are long and productive.

Soil-forming factors continue to affect soils during their existence, even on 'stable' landscapes that are long-enduring, some for millions of years. Materials are deposited on top and materials are blown or washed away from the surface. With additions, removals and alterations, soils are always subject to new conditions. Whether these are slow or rapid changes depend on climate, landscape position and biological activity.

Soil colour is often the first impression one has when viewing soil. Striking colours and contrasting patterns are especially memorable. The Red River (Mississippi watershed) carries sediment eroded from extensive reddish soils like Port Silt Loam in Oklahoma. The Yellow River in China carries yellow sediment from eroding loessal soils. Mollisols in the Great Plains are darkened and enriched by organic matter. Podsols in boreal forests have highly contrasting layers due to acidity and leaching. Soil colour is primarily influenced by soil mineralogy. Many soil colours are due to the extensive and various iron minerals. The development and distribution of colour in a soil profile result from chemical and biological weathering, especially redox reactions. As the primary minerals in soil parent material weather, the elements combine into new and colourful compounds. Iron forms secondary minerals with a yellow or red colour, organic matter decomposes into black and brown compounds, and manganese, sulfur and nitrogen can form black mineral deposits. These pigments produce various colour patterns due to effects by the environment during soil formation. Aerobic conditions produce uniform or gradual colour changes, while reducing environments result in disrupted colour flow with complex, mottled patterns and points of colour concentration.

Soil structure is the arrangement of soil particles into aggregates. These may have various shapes, sizes and degrees of development or expression. Soil structure affects aeration, water movement, resistance to erosion and plant root growth. Structure often gives clues to texture, organic matter content, biological activity, past soil evolution, human use, and chemical and mineralogical conditions under which the soil formed.

Soil texture refers to sand, silt and clay composition. Soil content affects soil behavior, including the retention capacity for nutrients and water. Sand and silt are the products of physical weathering, while clay is the product of chemical weathering. Clay content has retention capacity for nutrients and water. Clay soils resist wind and water erosion better than silty and sandy soils, because the particles are more tightly joined to each other. In medium-textured soils, clay is often translocated downward through the soil profile and accumulates in the subsoil.

The electrical resistivity of soil can affect the rate of galvanic corrosion of metallic structures in contact with the soil. Higher moisture content or increased electrolyte concentration can lower the resistivity and thereby increase the rate of corrosion. Soil resistivity values typically range from about 2 to 1000 O·m, but more extreme values are not unusual.

Soil Horizons

The naming of soil horizons is based on the type of material the horizons are composed of; these materials reflect the duration of the specific processes used in soil formation. They are labeled using a short hand notation of letters and numbers. They are described and classified by their colour, size, texture, structure, consistency, root quantity, pH, voids, boundary characteristics, and if they have nodules or concretions. Any one soil profile does not have all the major horizons covered below; soils may have few or many horizons.

The exposure of parent material to favorable conditions produces initial soils that are suitable for plant growth. Plant growth often results in the accumulation of organic residues, the accumulated organic layer is called the O horizon. Biological organisms colonize and break down organic materials, making available nutrients that other plants and animals can live on. After sufficient time a distinctive organic surface layer forms with humus which is called the A horizon.

Soil is classified into categories in order to understand relationships between different soils and to determine the usefulness of a soil for a particular use. One of the first classification systems was developed by the Russian scientist Dokuchaev around 1880. It was modified a number of times by American and European researchers, and developed into the system commonly used until the 1960s. It was based on the idea that soils have a particular morphology based on the materials and factors that form them. In the 1960s, a different classification system began to emerge, that focussed on soil morphology instead of parental materials and soil-forming factors. Since then it has undergone further modifications. The World Reference Base for Soil Resources (WRB) aims to establish an international reference base for soil classification.

Orders

Orders are the highest category of soil classification. Order types end in the letters sol. In the US classification system, there are ten orders:

- ***Entisol*** — recently formed soils that lack well-developed horizons. Commonly found on unconsolidated sediments like sand, some have an A horizon on top of bedrock.
- ***Vertisol*** — inverted soils. They tend to swell when wet and shrink upon drying, often forming deep cracks that surface layers can fall into.
- ***Inceptisol*** — young soils. They have subsurface horizon formation but show little eluviation and illuviation.
- ***Aridisol*** — dry soils forming under desert conditions. They include nearly 20 per cent of soils on Earth. Soil formation is slow, and accumulated organic matter is

scarce. They may have subsurface zones (calcic horizons) where calcium carbonates have accumulated from percolating water. Many aridiso soils have well-developed Bt horizons showing clay movement from past periods of greater moisture.

- ***Mollisol*** — soft soils with very thick A horizons.
- ***Spodosol*** — soils produced by podsolization. They are typical soils of coniferous and deciduous forests in cooler climates.
- ***Alfisol*** — soils with aluminium and iron. They have horizons of clay accumulation, and form where there is enough moisture and warmth for at least three months of plant growth.
- ***Ultisol*** — soils that are heavily leached.
- ***Oxisol*** — soil with heavy oxide content.
- ***Histosol*** — organic soils.

Most living things in soils, including plants, insects, bacteria and fungi, are dependent on organic matter for nutrients and energy. Soils often have varying degrees of organic compounds in different states of decomposition. Many soils, including desert and rocky-gravel soils, have no or little organic matter. Soils that are all organic matter, such as peat (histosols), are infertile.

Humus

Humus refers to organic matter that has decomposed to a point where it is resistant to further breakdown or alteration. Humic acids and fulvic acids are important constituents of humus and typically form from plant residues like foliage, stems and roots. After death, these plant residues begin to decay, starting the formation of humus. Humus formation involves changes within the soil and plant residue, there is a reduction of water soluble constituents including cellulose and hemicellulose; as the residues are deposited and break down, humin, lignin and lignin complexes accumulate within the soil; as microorganisms live and feed on the decaying plant matter, an increase in proteins occurs.

Lignin is resistant to breakdown and accumulates within the soil; it also chemically reacts with amino acids which add to its resistance to decomposition, including enzymatic decomposition by microbes. Fats and waxes from plant matter have some resistance to decomposition and persist in soils for a while. Clay soils often have higher organic contents that persist longer than soils without clay. Proteins normally decompose readily, but when bound to clay particles they become more resistant to decomposition. Clay particles also absorb enzymes that would break down proteins. The addition of organic matter to clay soils, can render the organic matter and any added nutrients inaccessible to plants and microbes for many years, since they can bind strongly to the clay. High soil tannin (polyphenol) content from plants can cause nitrogen to be sequestered by proteins or cause nitrogen immobilization, also making nitrogen unavailable to plants.

Humus formation is a process dependent on the amount of plant material added each year and the type of base soil; both are affected by climate and the type of organisms present. Soils with humus can vary in nitrogen content but have 3 to 6 per cent nitrogen typically; humus, as a reserve of nitrogen and phosphorus, is a vital component affecting soil fertility. Humus also absorbs water, acting as a moisture reserve, that plants can utilize; it also expands and shrinks between dry and wet states, providing pore spaces. Humus is less stable than other soil constituents, because it is affected by microbial decomposition, and over time its concentration decreases without the addition of new organic matter. However, some forms of humus are highly stable and may persist over centuries if not millennia: they are issued from the slow oxidation of charcoal, also called black carbon, like in Amazonian Terra preta or Black Earths, or from the sequestration of humic compounds within mineral horizons, like in podzols.

Climate and Organics

The production and accumulation or degradation of organic matter and humus is greatly dependent on climate conditions. Temperature and soil moisture are the major factors in the formation or degradation of organic matter, they along with topography, determine the formation of organic soils. Soils high in organic matter tend to form under wet or cold conditions where decomposer activity is impeded by low temperature or excess moisture.

Soil Solutions

Different soils, under varying conditions, have diverse colloidal solutions. These solutions exchange gases with the soil atmosphere. These solutions can contain dissolved sugars; fulvic acids and other organic acids; plant micronutrients such as zinc, iron and copper, plus other metals; ammonium plus a host of others. Some soils have sodium solutions that greatly impact plant growth, calcium is common in forest soils. Soil pH effects the type and amount of anions and cations that soil solutions contain and exchange with the soil atmosphere and biological organisms.

In Nature

Biogeography is the study of special variations in biological communities. Soils are a restricting factor as to which plants can grow in which environments. Soil scientists survey soils in the hope of understanding controls as to what vegetation can and will grow in a particular location.

Geologists also have a particular interest in the patterns of soil on the surface of the earth. Soil texture, colour and chemistry often reflect the underlying geologic parent material, and soil types often change at geologic unit boundaries. Buried paleosols mark previous land surfaces and record climatic conditions from previous eras. Geologists use this paleopedological record to understand the ecological relationships in past ecosystems. According to the theory of biorhexistasy, prolonged conditions conducive to forming deep, weathered soils result in increasing ocean salinity and the formation of limestone.

Geologists use soil profile features to establish the duration of surface stability in the context of geologic faults or slope stability. An offset subsoil horizon indicates rupture during soil formation and the degree of subsequent subsoil formation is relied upon to establish time since rupture.

Soil is used in agriculture, where it serves as the primary nutrient base for plants; however, as demonstrated by hydroponics, it is not essential to plant growth if the soil-contained nutrients could be dissolved in a solution. The types of soil used in agriculture (among other things, such as the purported level of moisture in the soil) vary with respect to the species of plants that are cultivated.

Soil material is a critical component in the mining and construction industries. Soil serves as a foundation for most construction projects. Massive volumes of soil can be involved in surface mining, road building and dam construction. Earth sheltering is the architectural practice of using soil for external thermal mass against building walls.

Soil resources are critical to the environment, as well as to food and fiber production. Soil provides minerals and water to plants. Soil absorbs rainwater and releases it later, thus preventing floods and drought. Soil cleans the water as it percolates. Soil is the habitat for many organisms: the major part of known and unknown biodiversity is in the soil, in the form of invertebrates (earthworms, woodlice, millipedes, centipedes, snails, slugs, mites, springtails, enchytraeids, nematodes, protists), bacteria, archaea, fungi and algae; and most organisms living above ground have part of them (plants) or spend part of their life cycle (insects) belowground. Above-ground and below-ground biodiversities are tightly interconnected, making soil protection of paramount importance for any restoration or conservation plan.

The biological component of soil is an extremely important carbon sink since about 57 per cent of the biotic content is carbon. Even on desert crusts, cyanobacteria lichens and mosses capture and sequester a significant amount of carbon by photosynthesis. Poor farming and grazing methods have degraded soils and released much of this sequestered carbon to the atmosphere. Restoring the world's soils could offset the huge increase in greenhouse gases causing global warming while improving crop yields and reducing water needs.

Waste management often has a soil component. Septic drain fields treat septic tank effluent using aerobic soil processes. Landfills use soil for daily cover.

Organic soils, especially peat, serve as a significant fuel resource; but wide areas of peat production, such as sphagnum bogs, are now protected because of patrimonial interest.

Both animals and humans in many cultures occasionally consume soil. It has been shown that some monkeys consume soil, together with their preferred food (tree foliage and fruits), in order to alleviate tannin toxicity.

Soils filter and purify water and affect its chemistry. Rain water and pooled water from ponds, lakes and rivers percolate through the soil horizons and the upper rock strata; thus becoming groundwater. Pests (viruses) and pollutants, such as persistent organic pollutants (chlorinated pesticides, polychlorinated biphenyls), oils (hydrocarbons), heavy metals (lead, zinc, cadmium), and excess nutrients (nitrates, sulfates, phosphates) are filtered out by the soil.

Soil organisms metabolize them or immobilize them in their biomass and necromass, thereby incorporating them into stable humus. The physical integrity of soil is also a prerequisite for avoiding landslides in rugged landscapes.

Land degradation is a human-induced or natural process which impairs the capacity of land to function. Soils are the critical component in land degradation when it involves acidification, contamination, desertification, erosion or salination.

While soil acidification of alkaline soils is beneficial, it degrades land when soil acidity lowers crop productivity and increases soil vulnerability to contamination and erosion. Soils are often initially acid because their parent materials were acid and initially low in the basic cations (calcium, magnesium, potassium and sodium). Acidification occurs when these elements are removed from the soil profile by normal rainfall, or the harvesting of forest or agricultural crops. Soil acidification is accelerated by the use of acid-forming nitrogenous fertilizers and by the effects of acid precipitation.

Soil contamination at low levels is often within soil capacity to treat and assimilate. Many waste treatment processes rely on this treatment capacity. Exceeding treatment capacity can damage soil biota and limit soil function. Derelict soils occur where industrial contamination or other development activity damages the soil to such a degree that the land cannot be used safely or productively. Remediation of derelict soil uses principles of geology, physics, chemistry and biology to degrade, attenuate, isolate or remove soil contaminants to restore soil functions and values. Techniques include leaching, air sparging, chemical amendments, phytoremediation, bioremediation and natural attenuation.

Desertification is an environmental process of ecosystem degradation in arid and semi-arid regions, often caused by human activity. It is a common misconception that droughts cause desertification. Droughts are common in arid and semiarid lands. Well-managed lands can recover from drought when the rains return. Soil management tools include maintaining soil nutrient and organic matter levels, reduced tillage and increased cover. These practices help to control erosion and maintain productivity during periods when moisture is available. Continued land abuse during droughts, however, increases land degradation. Increased population and livestock pressure on marginal lands accelerates desertification.

Soil erosional loss is caused by wind, water, ice and movement in response to gravity. Although the processes may be simultaneous, erosion is distinguished from weathering. Erosion is an intrinsic natural process, but in many places it is increased by human land use. Poor land use practices including deforestation, overgrazing and improper construction activity. Improved management can limit erosion by using techniques like limiting disturbance during construction, avoiding construction during erosion prone periods, intercepting runoff, terrace-building, use of erosion-suppressing cover materials, and planting trees or other soil binding plants.

A serious and long-running water erosion problem occurs in China, on the middle reaches of the Yellow River and the upper reaches of the Yangtze River. From the Yellow River, over 1.6-billion tons of sediment flow each year into the ocean. The sediment originates primarily from water erosion (gully erosion) in the Loess Plateau region of northwest China.

Soil piping is a particular form of soil erosion that occurs below the soil surface. It is associated with levee and dam failure, as well as sink hole formation. Turbulent flow removes soil starting from the mouth of the seep flow and subsoil erosion advances upgradient. The term sand boil is used to describe the appearance of the discharging end of an active soil pipe.

Soil salination is the accumulation of free salts to such an extent that it leads to degradation of soils and vegetation. Consequences include corrosion damage, reduced plant growth, erosion due to loss of plant cover and soil structure, and water quality problems due to sedimentation. Salination occurs due to a combination of natural and human caused processes. Arid conditions favor salt accumulation. This is especially apparent when soil parent material is saline. Irrigation of arid lands is especially problematic. All irrigation water has some level of salinity. Irrigation, especially when it involves leakage from canals, often raise the underlying water table. Rapid salination occurs when the land surface is within the capillary fringe of saline groundwater. Soil salinity control involves flushing with higher levels of applied water in combination with tile drainage.

9 Sowing

Sowing is the process of planting seeds.

Before sowing, certain seeds first require a treatment prior to the sowing process. This treatment may be seed scarification, stratification, seed soaking or seed cleaning with cold (or medium hot) water. Seed soaking is generally done by placing seeds in medium hot water for at least 24 to 48 hours. Seed cleaning is done especially with fruit (as the flesh of the fruit around the seed can quickly become prone to attack from insects or plagues. To clean the seed, usually seed rubbings with cloth/paper is performed, sometimes assisted with a seed washing. Seed washing is generally done by submerging cleansed seeds 20 minutes in 50 degree Celsius water. This (rather hot than moderately hot) water kills any organisms that may have survived on the skin of a seed. Especially with easily infected tropical fruit such as lychees and rambutans, seed washing with high temperature water is vital.

In addition to the mentioned seed pretreatments, seed germination is also assisted when disease-free soil is used. Especially when trying to germinate difficult seed (e.g. certain tropical fruit), prior treatment of the soil (along with the usage of the most suitable soil; e.g. potting soil, prepared soil or other substrates) is vital. The two most used soil treatments are pasteurisation and sterilisation. Depending on the necessity, pasteurisation is to be preferred as this does not kill all organisms. Sterilisation can be done when trying to grow truly difficult crops. To pasteurise the soil, the soil is heated for 15 minutes in an oven of 120 °C.

Plants Which Are Usually Sown

Among the major field crops, oats, wheat, and rye are sowed, grasses and legumes are seeded, and maize and soybeans are planted. In planting, wider rows (generally 75 cm (30 in) or more) are used, and the intent is to have precise, even spacing between individual seeds in the row; various mechanisms have been devised to count out individual seeds at exact intervals.Difference between sowing and planting must not be forgotten.

Sowing Depth

In seeding, little if any soil is placed over the seeds. More precisely, seeds can be generally sown into the soil by maintaining a planting depth of about 2-3 times the size of the seed.

Sowing Types and Patterns

For hand sowing, several sowing types exist; these include

- Flat sowing
- Ridge sowing
- Wide bed sowing

Several patterns for sowing may be used together with these types; these include:

Regular Rows

Rows that are indented at the even rows (so that the seeds are placed in a crossed pattern). This method is much better, as more light may fall on the seedlings as they come out.

Hand Sowing

Hand sowing is the process of casting handfuls of seed over prepared ground: broadcasting. Usually, a drag or harrow is employed to incorporate the seed into the soil. Though labour intensive for any but small areas, this method is still used in some situations. Practice is required to sow evenly and at the desired rate. A hand seeder can be used for sowing, though it is less of a help than it is for the smaller seeds of grasses and legumes.

Hand sowing may be combined with pre-sowing in seed trays. This allows the plants to come to strength indoors during cold periods (eg spring in temperate countries).

In agriculture, most seed is now sown using a seed drill, which offers greater precision; seed is sown evenly and at the desired rate. The drill also places the seed at a measured distance below the soil, so that less seed is required. The standard design uses a fluted feed metering system, which is volumetric in nature; individual seeds are not counted. Rows are typically about 10-30 cm apart, depending on the crop species and growing conditions. Several row opener types are used depending on soil type and local tradition. Grain drills are most often drawn by tractors, but can also be pulled by horses. Pick-up trucks are sometimes used, since little draft is required.

A seed rate of about 100 kg of seed per hectare (2 bushels per acre) is typical, though rates vary considerably depending on crop species, soil conditions, and farmer's preference. Excessive rates can cause the crop to lodge, while too thin a rate will result in poor utilisation of the land, competition with weeds and a reduction in the yield.

Open Field

Open-field refers to the form of sowing used historically in the agricultural context whereby fields are prepared generically and left open, as the name suggests, before being sown directly with seed. The seed is frequently left uncovered at the surface of the soil before germinating and therefore exposed to the prevailing climate and conditions. This is in contrast to the seedbed method used more commonly in domestic gardening or more specific (modern) agricultural scenarios where the seed is applied beneath the soil surface and monitored and manually tended frequently to ensure more successful growth rates and better yields.

Tillage

Tillage is the agricultural preparation of the soil by ploughing, ripping, or turning it. Tillage can also mean the land that is tilled. There are two types of tillage: primary and secondary tillage.

Intensive Tillage

Intensive tillage systems leave less than 15 per cent crop residue cover less than 500 pounds per acre (560 kg/ha) of small grain residue. These types of tillage systems are often referred to as conventional tillage systems but as reduced and conservation tillage systems have been more widely adopted, it is often not appropriate to refer to this type of system as conventional. These systems involve often multiple operations with implements such as a mold board, disk, and/or chisel plow. Then a finisher with a harrow, rolling basket, and cutter can be used to prepare the seed bed. There are many variations.

Reduced Tillage

Reduced tillage systems leave between 15 and 30 per cent residue cover on the soil or 500 to 1000 pounds per acre (560 to 1100 kg/ha) of small grain residue during the critical erosion period. This may involve the use of a chisel plow, field cultivators, or other implements. See the general comments below to see how they can affect the amount of residue.

Conservation Tillage

Conservation tillage systems are methods of soil tillage which leave a minimum of 30 per cent of crop residue on the soil surface or at least 1,000 lb/ac (1,100 kg/ha) of small grain residue on the surface during the critical soil erosion period. This slows water movement, which reduces the amount of soil erosion. Conservation tillage systems also benefit farmers by reducing fuel consumption and soil compaction. By reducing the number of times the farmer travels over the field, farmers realize significant savings in fuel and labour. Conservation tillage was used on about 38 per cent, 109,000,000 acres (440,000 km^2), of all US cropland, 293,000,000 acres (1,190,000 km^2) planted as of 2004 according to the USDA.

However, conservation tillage systems delay warming of the soil due to the reduction of dark earth exposure to the warmth of the spring sun, thus delaying the planting of the next year's spring crop.

- No-till
- Strip-Till
- Mulch-Till
- Ridge-Till

Purposes of Tillage

Plowing loosens and aerates the soil which in turn facilitates deeper penetration of roots. A drawback is the compaction of the lower layers of soil.

It helps in the growth of microorganisms present in the soil and thus, maintains the fertility of the soil, though fertility can decline as microorganisms' boom period after tilling is followed by a bust period. It is debatable whether worms benefit or suffer from tillage.

It helps in the mixing of organic matter (humus) and nutrients evenly throughout the soil.

It is used for destroying weeds.

General Comments

The type of implement makes the most difference, although other factors can have an effect.

Tilling in absolute darkness (night tillage) might reduce the number of weeds that sprout following the tilling operation by half. Light is necessary to break the dormancy of some weed species' seed, so if fewer seeds are exposed to light during the tilling process, fewer will sprout. This may help reduce the amount of herbicides needed for weed control.

Greater speeds, when using certain tillage implements (disks and chisel plows), lead to more intensive tillage (i.e., less residue is on the soil surface).

Increasing the angle of disks causes residues to be buried more deeply. Increasing their concavity makes them more aggressive.

Chisel plows can have spikes or sweeps. Spikes are more aggressive.

Percentage residue is used to compare tillage systems because the amount of crop residue affects the soil loss due to erosion.

Definitions

Primary tillage loosens the soil and mixes in fertilizer and/or plant material, resulting in soil with a rough texture.

Secondary tillage produces finer soil and sometimes shapes the rows. It can be done by an using various combinations of equipment: plough, disk plough, harrow, dibble, hoe, shovel, rotary tillers, subsoiler, ridge or bed forming tillers, roller.

Weed plants (seeds, tubers, etc.) may be exhausted by repeated tilling. The weeds expend energy to reach the surface, and then get turned into the soil by tilling. The cycle is repeated until the weeds are dead.

History of Tilling

Tilling was first performed via human labour, sometimes involving slaves. Hoofed animals could also be used to till soil via trampling. The wooden plow was then invented. It could be pulled by mule, ox, elephant, water buffalo, or similar sturdy animal. Horses are generally unsuitable, though breeds such as the Clydesdale could work. The steel plow allowed farming in the American Midwest, where tough prairie grasses and rocks caused trouble. Soon after 1900, the farm tractor was introduced, which eventually made modern large-scale agriculture possible.

Alternatives to Tilling

Modern agricultural science has greatly reduced the use of tillage. Crops can be grown for several years without any tillage through the use of herbicides to control weeds, crop varieties that tolerate packed soil, and equipment that can plant seeds or fumigate the soil without really digging it up. This practice, called no-till farming, reduces costs and environmental change by reducing soil erosion and diesel fuel usage (although it does require the use of herbicides). Most organic farming tends to require extensive tilling, as did most farming throughout history, although researchers are investigating farming in polyculture that would eliminate the need for both tillage and pesticides, such as no-dig gardening.

10 Integrated Farming

Integrated farming (or integrated agriculture) is a commonly and broadly used word to explain a more integrated approach to farming as compared to existing monoculture approaches. It refers to agricultural systems that integrate livestock and crop production and may sometimes be known as Integrated Biosystems.

While not often considered as part of the permaculture movement Integrated Farming is a similar 'whole systems approach' to agriculture. There have been efforts to link the two together such as at the 2007 International Permaculture Conference in Brazil. Agro-ecology (which was developed at University of California Santa Cruz) and Bio-dynamic farming also describe similar integrated approaches.

Examples include:

- 'pig tractor' systems where the animals are confined in crop fields well prior to planting and 'plow' the field by digging for roots
- poultry used in orchards or vineyards after harvest to clear rotten fruit and weeds while fertilizing the soil
- cattle or other livestock allowed to graze cover crops between crops on farms that contain both cropland and pasture (or where transhumance is employed)

Water based agricultural systems that provide way for effective and efficient recycling of farm nutrients producing fuel, fertilizer and a compost tea/mineralized irrigation water in the process.

ZERI

Zero Emissions Research and Initiatives (formed in 1994) developed a similar approach to FARRE seeking to promote agricultural and industrial production models that sought to incorporate nature's wisdom into the process. ZERI helped support an effort by an environmental engineer from Mauritius named George Chan.

George Chan

Chan working with a network of poly-culture farming pioneers began refining Integrated Farming practices that had already been developed in south-east Asia in the 1960 through the 1980s, building on traditional night soil farming practice. In China, programmes embracing this form of integrated farming have been successful in demonstrating how an intensive growing systems can use organic and sustainable farming practices, while providing high agriculture yields.

Taking what he learned from the Chinese during his time there, Chan worked at the UN University in the 1990s and forwarded an approach to Integrated Farming which was termed Integrated Biomass Systems working specifically under the UNU/ZERI ZERI Bag Programme.

Chan during his work with UNU sought to make the case that Integrated Biomass Systems were well suited to help small island nations and low lying tropical regions become more self-reliant and prosperous in the production of food. Working with ZERI, he developed several prototypes for this approach around the world including sites in Namibia and Fiji. The scientifically verified results in a UNDP sponsored congress in 1997 resulted in the adoption of the IBS by the State Government of Paraná, Brazil where dozens of piggeries have applied the system generating food, energy while improving health and environmental conditions.

ZERI Bag had a significant African component that included assisting Father Godfrey Nzamujo in the development of the Songhai Farm Integrated Farming project in Benin.

Farm

A farm is an area of land, including various structures, devoted primarily to the practice of producing and managing food (produce, grains, or livestock), fibres and, increasingly, fuel. It is the basic production facility in food production. Farms may be owned and operated by a single individual, family, community, corporation or a company. A farm can be a holding of any size from a fraction of a hectare to several thousand hectares.

The word came via French *ferme* from Late Latin *firma* = 'fixed payment' from Latin *firmus* = 'firm, solid', and originally referred to a big landowner farming out his land among other men to run it, rather than running it all himself. As times have changed fewer people are needed to assist in running the farm because of the increase of mechanization.

History

The practice of agriculture first began around 8000 BC in the Fertile Crescent of Mesopotamia (part of present day Iraq, Turkey, Syria and Jordan which was then greener).

The development of farming and farms was an important component in establishing towns. Once people have moved from hunting and/or gathering and from simple horticulture to active farming, social arrangements of roads, distribution, collection, and marketing can evolve. With the exception of plantations and colonial farms, farm sizes tend to be small in newly-settled lands and expand as transportation and markets become sophisticated.

Farming

The term farming covers a wide spectrum of agricultural production work. At one end of this spectrum is the subsistence farmer, who farms a small area with limited resource inputs, and produces only enough food to meet the needs of his/her family. At the other end is commercial intensive agriculture, including industrial agriculture. Such farming involves large fields and/or numbers of animals, large resource inputs (pesticides, fertilizers, etc.), and a high level of mechanization. These operations generally attempt to maximize financial income from grain, produce, or livestock.

Traditionally, the goal of farming was to work collectively as a community to grow and harvest crops that could be grown in mass such as wheat, corn, squash, and other cash crops. Centuries later these same farmers took charge of livestock, and began growing food exclusively for the feeding of livestock as well as for the community. With the growth of actual civilization the farmer's focus changed from basic survival to that of financial gain. In smaller towns on the outset of civilization the farmer did retain the need to grow their own food, but the financially minded farmer was largely spreading. With the Renaissance came the plantation, a 'Farm' primarily worked by others primarily for the gain of the plantation's owner.

Types of Farms

A business producing tree fruits or nuts is called an *orchard*; a *vineyard* produces grapes. The *stable* is used for operations principally involved in the training of horses. Stud and commercial farms breed and produce other animals and livestock. A farm that is primarily used for the production of milk and dairy is a *dairy farm*. A *market garden* or *truck farm* is a farm that grows vegetables, but little or no grain. Additional specialty farms include fish farms, which raise fish in captivity as a food source, and tree farms, which grow trees for sale for transplant, lumber, or decorative use. A plantation is usually a large farm or estate, on which cotton, tobacco, coffee or sugar cane, are cultivated, usually by resident labourers.

Farm produce on display at an agricultural show, NSW.

Types of farming:

- Collective farming
- Factory farming
- Intensive farming
- Protected culture farming
- Organic farming
- Vertical farming
- Fell farming

Dairy farming is a class of agriculture, where female cattle, goats, or other mammals are raised for their milk, which may be either processed on-site or transported to a dairy for processing and eventual retail sale.

In most Western countries, a centralized dairy facility processes milk and dairy products, such as cream, butter, and cheese. In the United States, these dairies are usually local companies, while in the southern hemisphere facilities may be run by very large nationwide or trans-national corporations (such as Fonterra).

Dairy farms generally sell the male calves borne by their mothers for veal meat, as dairy breeds are not normally satisfactory for commercial beef production. Many dairy farms also grow their own feed, typically including corn, alfalfa, and hay. This is fed directly to the cows, or stored as silage for use during the winter season. Additional dietary supplements are added to the feed to improve milk production.

Farm control and ownership has traditionally been a key indicator of status and power, especially in agrarian societies. The distribution of farm ownership has historically been closely linked to form of government. Medieval feudalism was essentially a system that centralized control of farmland, control of farm labor and political power, while the early American democracy, in which land ownership was a prerequisite for voting rights, was built on relatively easy paths to individual farm ownership. However, the gradual modernization and mechanization of farming, which greatly increases both the efficiency and capital requirements of farming, has led to increasingly large farms owned by individuals or corporations. This has usually been accompanied by the decoupling of political power from farm ownership.

Forms of Ownership

In some societies (especially socialist and communist), collective farming is the norm, with either government ownership of the land or common ownership by a local group. Especially in societies without widespread industrialized farming, tenant farming and sharecropping are common; farmers either pay landowners for the right to use farmland or give up a portion of the crops.

FARMS AROUND THE WORLD

Australia

Farming is a significant economic sector in Australia. A farm is an area of land used for primary production which will include buildings.

Where most of the income is from some other employment, and the farm is really an expanded residence, the term *hobby farm* is common. This will allow sufficient size for recreational use but be very unlikely to produce sufficient income to be self-sustaining. Hobby farms are commonly around 5 acres (20,000 m^2) but may be much larger depending upon land prices (which vary regionally).

Often very small farms used for intensive primary production are referred to by the specialization they are being used for, such as a dairy rather than a dairy farm, a piggery, a market garden, etc. This also applies to feedlots, which are specifically developed to a single purpose and are often not able to be used for more general purpose (mixed) farming practices.

In remote areas farms can become quite large. As with *estates* in England, there is no defined size or method of operation at which a large farm becomes a station.

Regardless of size, the term *station* is only used for farms where the main activity is grazing. Some cotton farms in north-western New South Wales or south-western Queensland have been formed by combining previous sheep stations once sufficient water has become available to allow cotton to be grown.

In the UK, *farm* as an agricultural unit, always denotes the area of pasture and other fields together with its farmhouse, farmyard and outbuildings. Very large farms, or groups of farms under the same ownership, may be called an estate. Conversely, a small farm surrounding the owner's dwelling is called a smallholding and is generally focussed on self-sufficiency with only the surplus being sold.

North America

The land and buildings of a farm are called the 'farmstead'. Enterprises where livestock are raised on rangeland are called *ranches.* Where livestock are raised in confinement on feed produced elsewhere, the term *feedlot* is usually used.

In the United States, eighty-one per cent of all farmworkers are migrant workers, and seventy-one per cent are foreign-born. Eighty per cent of farmworkers are men, with the average age being 31. Additionally, farmworkers earn less than $75,000 per year, making an average hourly rate of less than $27.00. On average, farmworker families earn $10,000 per year, which is significantly below the 2005 U.S. poverty level of $19,874 for a family of four.

11 Biomass Gasifier Systems

Biomass fuels continue to play an important role both in the domestic and industrial sector in India, as it is an agricultural - based economy. Biomass is the main source of energy for a large number of small, rural, and cottage industries along with the majority of rural households. The majority of these enterprises belong to an unstructured sector and hence information and data on these industries are scarce. These industries provide employment to millions of people and form a very important part of the rural economy. The biomass-consuming industries can be divided into two categories, namely traditional industries and new or otential industries.

Traditional biomass-based industries are essentially rural cottage and small-scale industries. These industries depend predominantly on biomass fuels such as wood, agricultural residues, and animal dung because biomass is cheap and its supply is assured. Biomass energy is used in these industries for direct heating (firing of bricks, lime), indirect firing (drying, baking), boiling, steam raising and distillation. New or potential biomass-based industries include many medium and small-sized enterprises that currently use fossil fuels and are willing to switch over, at least partially, to biomass fuels available locally at lower prices. Examples of these industries include textile mills, brick kilns, mini cement plants, steel re-rolling and lime kilns. This situation calls for the development of a biomass-based but energy efficient and environment friendly system with better environmental acceptability, economic viability, and good process control. The biomass gasifier system is ideal for such applications as it can offer all these qualities.

Biomass gasification is the process of conversion, through partial combustion of solid biomass feed material into combustible gas. The technology may be regarded as fuel switching to convert solid fuel to gaseous fuel. Gasification is achieved in the presence of heat and a limited supply of oxygen, resulting in incomplete combustion of the solid biomass material. The resulting combustible gas mixture can be burnt directly in an oven/burner for thermal applications or cooled, cleaned and fed into a diesel engine to generate electricity. For over two decades, TERI (The Energy and Resources Institute) has been working on the development of various biomass gasifier designs (downdraft, updraft and natural draft) both thermal applications as well as for decentralized power generation. So far, more than 350 TERI gasifier systems have been successfully installed in the field throughout India with a cumulative installed capacity of over 13 MWth. This chapter gives an account of TERI's efforts in developing and promoting biomass gasification as a sustainable and eco-friendly option to meet energy demand for three selected rural applications: cardamom drying, arecanut processing and community cooking.

Gasifier System for Community Cooking

In a developing country like India, biomass is still and will remain the major fuel for cooking energy. There are several residential schools and religious places that consume substantial quantities of fuelwood daily. Apart from contributing to deforestation, it also consumes a lot of time and labour in its collection. TERI has designed both downdraft and updraft gasifier based cooking systems and installed these at residential tribal schools at Doimukh in Arunachal Pradesh and Kankia in Orissa. The updraft gasifier system can also be operated without a blower under natural draft mode in unelectrifi ed villages. The fuel consumption data and time required for cooking using the gasifier system is along with a comparison to the traditional stove.

Wood Gas System for Large Cardamom Curing

With an annual production capacity of more than 4000 Metric Tonnes (MT), India is the largest producer of large cardamom with a 54 per cent share in world production, followed by Nepal and Bhutan. Within India more than 85 per cent of production comes from Sikkim and Darjeeling. To achieve a long storage time and to bring out the characteristic aroma, cardamom capsules have to be dried to reduce the moisture content from about 70-80 per cent to below 10 per cent.

Traditionally, an inefficient smoking method is employed, using a bhatti (oven) system. Out of the total large cardamom cultivation area in Sikkim, more than 85 per cent plantations are very small with an area of less than 2 ha, with over 34,000 traditional bhattis, making it a small farmer's business. The bhatti is made-up of locally available construction materials. It has a 0.60 m thick stonewall structure on three sides and a wide opening in the front for burning large wood logs.

About 400-600 kg fresh, large-cardamom capsules are loaded as a thick bed on a bamboo or wiremesh platform and placed on the stonewalls. Large wood logs from within plantations are fed and burnt in the front opening of the bhatti, and the capsules are exposed to a large amount of smoke to dry them. Thus the cardamom bed is exposed to the thick smoke generated during the burning of wet wood and it takes about 30-50 hours to dry the cardamom (Mande et al. 1999). TERI has developed an appropriate gasifier-based large-cardamom dryer system to suit local conditions. The system is made of locally available material and can be easily transported into remote forested areas where cardamom plantations are found. More than 150 systems have been installed in the state in collaboration with the state Horticulture Department and these systems have also been pilot tested in Nagaland state in India, as well as in Nepal and Bhutan. Through extensive field performance monitoring it was observed that use of gasifier not only resulted in more than 62 per cent fuelwood saving but also resulted in improving the quality of the product, as the dried cardamom retained 35 per cent more volatile oils and natural reddish colour. Thus induction of a gasifier system cannot only help in the preservation of natural forest but also in increasing the income for farmers. A greater oil content without a burnt smell could also open new industries for large-cardamom by way of extracting its oil.

Arecanut Processing

Arecanut palm (Areca catechu L.) is cultivated for its kernel, which is chewed in its tender, ripe or processed form. The north-eastern region of India is a major producer of arecanut in India, producing 21 per cent of the total national production. Most of the production is exported to outside the region. The major processing clusters are in northeast India with large (5-7 tonnes of processed arecanut produced weekly) and medium sized (2-3 tonne of processed arecanut produced weekly) units located in Rupahi and Howly, in the state of Assam. Apart from these clusters, thousands of cottage-level processing units are also found in Cachar, Karimganj, Darrang, Dhubri and Kokrajhar districts of Assam. There are two varieties of processed arecanut processed in the state of Assam and other states in India: Boiled, dried nuts (red in colour, called chikni) and non-boiled, sun dried nuts (called supari). Tender green arecanut are dehusked, boiled and dried to obtain the chikni. Boiling is done in batches in flat, open, iron pans (4-5 feet diameter) where chopped nut pieces are mixed with colour and boiled at 70-80 °C, to cook and absorb the colour.

The first batch of boiling in a day takes 50 minutes and subsequent batches take 30 minutes. Though the nuts should be boiled for 20 minutes to get a good quality boiled nut, owners restrict the boiling time to save the scarce fuelwood. The drying (slow eating) is done in brick-cement/ brick-mud frame sheds (7 feet height and 7.5 feet width) with vertical partitions. Thick bamboo mats are used to spread the chopped nuts out for drying and wood is fired in each partition on the ground, well below the bamboo mats. In the large and medium sized units, fire curing is initially done for 12 hours at a temperature of 70-75 °C and then the dried product is further sun dried for 2-3 days to remove any residual moisture. On average 100 to 150 kg fuelwood is used to produce 100 kg of processed arecanut, of which 60 per cent is used for boiling and the rest for drying. The average wood-burning rate for boiling is 115 kg per hour, with SFC (specific fuel consumption) of 0.70 kg wood per kg boiled nut. Detailed water boiling tests carried out on the vessel-bhatti combination currently used, revealed that the useful power requirement is 30-35 kWth. TERI has successfully developed an integrated gasifier-based system for boiling, as well as drying, and has successfully demonstrated the application in the Rupahi cluster. The gasifier with a wood consumption rate of about 20 kg/hr capacity, was used for boiling arecanut in the xisting boiling pan and also utilized the hot flue gases for drying. The gasifier could also be operated successfully using waste arecanut husk (a by-product during de-husking operation) that makes the gasifier option even more attractive. Further improvements in energy efficiency are achieved by utilizing the hot gases or drying instead of traditionally burning fuelwood. Biomass gasification technology can help in taking a rural population using biomass as a fuel two steps up on energy ladder (from solid to gaseous fuel). Application of gasifier for heat applications in rural areas has significant fuel saving potential coupled with other benefits such as improving the working environment, improving product quality and processing rates, due to controlled burning of gaseous fuel obtained through gasification of solid biomass.

12 Backyard Cash Crops

Many large farms have had trouble making a profit in the past few years. However, there are several good ways to make money farming small gardens plots. Thousands of people are using these methods to earn part-time or full-time incomes. This report will outline several profitable ways that you can use to quickly begin producing cash crops. Don't misunderstand, I'm not talking about growing common crops like tomatoes and so forth. No. The secret of cash crops from small gardens is growing special, hard-to-find products that will bring you premium prices. And, in many cases, the demand far outstrips the supply for these crops. You'll also learn how to open a small roadside stand selling common and special vegetables and fruits. Something else. You'll not have to engage in 'backbreaking' labour. While there is some amount of work required, there are techniques that can reduce the amount of labour once you are established. For example: raspberries can be heavily mulched each year to eliminate future weeds. Business overview raising backyard crops is a fairly easy business to set up and operate. You'll need at least half acre of ground. Preferably, one acre or more. Then you'll need to master the gardening techniques for growing top quality crops. After that, it's simply a matter of choosing how you want to market your crops for cash.

Profit Potential

How much money can you earn with this type of business? It depends on several factors, including: crop selection, quality of your crop, amount of acreage planted, crop yields, and effective marketing. Your earnings can vary from $2,000 per acre up to $20,000 per acre each year with the specialty crops described in this report. So this is not a business that can make you rich 'overnight', but with several profitable acres your income can be good to excellent.

Keys to Success

There are several keys to success in this type of business. They are:

1. Plan ahead to grow the best kinds of crops for the amount of space you have, and type of soil and climate in your location.
2. Learn the best growing techniques (and easiest methods) for producing high yield crops.
3. Buy the best seeds, bulbs, trees, and vines and plant them in the proper manner.
4. Learn good marketing skills for selling the crops.

These simple, and obvious steps are easy to take. Anyone can successfully raise cash producing crops with a little effort. Of course, some labour is involved in preparing the ground like weeding, trimming, packing and selling. However, some of these cash crops require less attention than common crops. Also, you could employ a high school student for one or two days per week to help out with portions of the work. Raising cash crops is also a very low risk and low cost business to start. In most cases, your start up costs can be $100 to $200 (or less) if you already own a suitable section of land. So you are risking very little money and you should always get some cash return even in a poor growing season.

Tools Needed

You do not need a wide array of expensive tools at the start. A shovel, hoes, wheelbarrow, seeds, plants and fertilizer are about all that is needed. However, it's quite handy to have (or have access to) a five horsepower rototiller. A tiller is a powerful assistant in the upkeep and preparation of your garden. And, of course, you'll also want to purchase, or borrow, a few books about specific gardening techniques in your area and for the specific crop you'll be growing. You'll find some excellent guides in the Source section of this booklet.

Land

How much land do you need to produce cash crops? In part, this will depend upon what you want to do. There are three different sizes of land that can be used:

1. less than one acre;
2. one to two acres;
3. six to twenty acres.

The size of your garden determines what your best crops will be in order to produce the most cash. For example: if you have one acre or less, you won't want to try growing apple and peach trees. You need more space for fruit trees. Instead, focus on crops like asparagus, strawberries, raspberries, herbs and other similar crops that can produce large amounts in small spaces. The other important factor is the type of soil in your area. Most crops require certain kinds of soil to produce the highest yield and the best quality. The good news is that you can improve your soil by using fertilizers. I recommend that you use natural types of fertilizers, such as horse/cow/chicken manure, and limit (or, best of all, eliminate) the amount of chemical fertilizers you use. Most of your customers will prefer 'organically grown' produce. Since most 'store bought' produce is usually laced with some kind of chemical, featuring organically grown crops can assure you of increased sales. There's always a market for health oriented produce. A great way to improve your soil is by composting. Composting turns leaves, grass clippings, scrap food, and other organic material into a rich soil. There are both long and short procedures for producing compost. Here's how.

Pick a spot for a compost pile (4 x 4 or 6 x 6 feet) and begin by putting down a 4 to 5 inch layer of leaves or grass clippings. Cover with an inch or so of dirt and a shovel-full or two of manure. Then start another layer of organic matter. Continue in this manner until the pile is 3 or 4 feet high. You can sprinkle each layer lightly with water. If you like, you can construct an enclosed wire 'box' for this compost pile. If you want to use the protracted method for composting, simply let the pile 'cook' for about 9 months. If you want a 'faster' compost wait 8 to 9 days then mix the pile. Then wait 3 or 4 days and mix again. Do this until the pile has turned into a rich soil-like mixture. This compost can then be worked into your soil. The purpose of composting is to develop heat and moisture within the pile. This will cause the organic matter to decompose into components that are usable by the plants. It will produce a lot of nitrogen-rich material as well as material rich loaded with minerals. You may need to add a cup of lime or bone meal between the layers of the pile to make an even better compost. You should have your soil tested to determine its acid, nitrogen, and mineral condition, or content. You'll then be able to determine what to add to the soil to correct any deficiencies. You'll also be able to determine what grows best in your type of soil. There are low cost soil testing kits available, or you can find local testing groups, such as your local county extension office or the agriculture department at most colleges.

Most of the small cash crop growers I've talked with use a rototiller for preparing the soil. If the soil has never been used for a garden, you should have it worked up good with a tractor the first year. After that, a rototiller can do the job. Of course, if you have more than a one acre garden you may still want to save a lot of work and hire someone with a tractor to plow your soil. You should find several full time and part time farmers advertising in the classified section of your local newspaper for their tilling services. The better prepared your soil is, the better the results will be. So take the time to find out the soil's current condition, add plenty of fertilizing material and work the soil up in preparation for planting. Crop selection is largely a matter of preference and how you want to market your product. For example, some products can easily be sold only locally while other products can be sold nationally as well as locally. Herbs are examples of produce that can be sold both ways. I recommend that you don't just plant one type of crop unless you have signed contracts to sell that crop, or have plenty of marketing experience. There are some exceptions to this rule: for example, specialized crops such as mushrooms and bamboo. Planting more than one type of produce will help avoid problems if something doesn't produce as well as expected, or if the market becomes saturated. Using good mulching techniques will help to eliminate weeds and lessen the amount of labour you'll need to put into the garden. It will also keep the soil around your plants moist and produce stronger plants. Almost all successful small cash crop growers use the mulching method.

Small Fruits

There are tremendous opportunities for part time fruit growers. Every large metropolitan area could use more fruit producers. This section will focus on the basic small fruit crops, such as blueberries, raspberries and strawberries. These fruits generally produce an excellent return on your investment. Much of the demand is for 'U-Pick' fields near larger cities. Thus, a few acres of small fruits can produce a substantial income. Except for strawberries, most of the fruit plants can keep producing for as long as 10 years, or more. Also, small fruit crops produce a high return per acre — up to $15,000 gross income per acre. Blueberries grow on small bushes and require an acid type soil. You can get about 1,000 bushes on an acre. Many farmers argue that blueberries are the best crop for 'U-Pick' operations. But blueberries take a little more care and careful adjustment of the soil acidity, and are a bit harder to grow than other berries. Yet once you have a good established stand of blueberries, they can produce an excellent income. Grapes can be grown almost anywhere there is fertile, well drained soil. Grapevines will last decades (up to 80 years!) and, therefore, can produce a permanent income. Grapes can be used in 'U-Pick' operations, and also sold via retail stores. It's important to study the proper pruning methods for grapes. Further information can be gleaned from U.S. Government agriculture publications found in most libraries or from the U.S. Government Printing Office in Washington, DC.

Raspberries can produce quick results and will continue producing for many years. The plants are low cost to purchase and establish, have little disease problems, and usually produce large crops. Best of all, there simply aren't enough of these delicious berries available. Thus, the demand is high and they will bring a large price per quart. You can easily propagate new plants yourself, adding to your crop each year. Raspberries require lots of sun, fertile, well drained soil, and effective mulching. Strawberries are also an extremely popular crop. You can easily sell all you grow either by the 'U-Pick' arrangement or sell direct to the consumer. The cost to establish a strawberry patch is generally low. And yields range from 6,000 to 15,000 pounds per acre. Here are a few tips for 'U-Pick' operations:

1. Have adequate parking, signs, and portable restrooms available.
2. Send each picker into assigned rows.

3. Use reusable containers and sell by the container, instead of by the pound.
4. Have plenty of empty containers to use, and make your customers feel at home.

Some growers are also producing other types of lesser-known crops such as kiwi, guavas, and Chinese dates. But, for most people just starting in the 'cash crop' business, the four small fruits recommended in this section are the most cost effective.

Flowers

There are several different ways to make profits from flowers: selling flower bulbs, cut flowers, and flower plants. These can be sold in a variety of wholesale and retail ways. A sizable flower business can be built upon half acre or less. Thus, flowers are an excellent choice if you have very little space. Here are a few examples of the most popular types of flowers:

1. Bulbs — canna, crocus, daffodils, gladiolus, iris, lilies, tulips.
2. Cut flowers — carnations, chrysanthemums, roses, snapdragons.
3. Live flowers — roses, violets, wildflowers, and virtually all other types of flowers.

Recently, a USDA horticulturist stated that the production of flowers is the fastest growing agriculture business today. The demand far outstrips the supply. A great way to start making money from flowers is by building a greenhouse. You can then grow plants for selling to the many retail outlets that sell flowers in the spring. A number of people have reported that they completely paid for a $7,000 - $10,000 greenhouse in just one season using this method. Flowers are always popular and will remain so. If you want to get into this business, you must become knowledgeable. And, more importantly, you must have or develop a love for flowers.

Herbs

Herb crops can be divided into 3 primary groupings. (There are some herbs that may fit into more than one of the following categories.)

1. Culinary herbs — used for flavorings, or as food.
2. Fragrant herbs — used for scents, potpourris, and sachets.
3. Medicinal — herbs used for as herbal remedies.

Herbs are continually becoming more in demand. The demand outstrips the current domestic supply, thus there is plenty of opportunity for growing and selling herbs. It's a pleasant business that costs little to start, takes little space and can produce a substantial income. One of the best things about herbs is that you can produce a fair amount of income per acre. Some growers produce as much as $12,000 - $15,000 per acre. Another important fact is that almost all areas of the United States are suitable for growing some type of herbs. Most herb crops can begin producing incomes in the same year they are planted. Therefore, you can plan a herb crop this winter and reap the profits next fall! You can find sources for herb plants and seeds by looking through the various gardening and farming magazines. Publications like, The Mother Earth News, Fine Gardening, Harrowsmith and Organic Gardening contain many ads for herb suppliers. Look in both the classified and display ad sections.

Herbs can be sold in a wide variety of ways:

1. Direct to the customer as plants.
2. Direct to the customer as a finished product.
3. Wholesaling to retail stores.
4. Wholesaling to bulk herb buyers.
5. Wholesaling to arts and crafts people who use the herbs in other products.
6. Fresh herbs to restaurants.

If you wish to become involved in growing herbs for profit, the first thing to do is to educate yourself about the different herbs. You'll discover that some herbs take special growing conditions to flourish. Then devise a plan to detail what herbs you will grow and how you'll market them. Here are a few examples of some popular herbs from the three classes listed earlier.

1. Culinary herbs — Basil, sage, chives, dill, parsley, mints, savory, rosemary, thyme.
2. Fragrant herbs — mints, tansy, clove, rue, thyme, rosemary, chamomile.
3. Medicinal herbs — borage, catnip, ginseng, gold seal, lobelia, pennyroyal, valerian.

Most successful herb growers plant a variety of herbs. They also use several different marketing techniques, such as: direct to the consumer, selling herb plants to other growers, and selling to restaurants. Dried herbs can also be sold by mail order. A few herb growers concentrate on one or two varieties for which there is a big demand. Examples include: peppermint and catnip. Usually, they already have contracts for selling the product to large wholesalers or companies that use the herbs in their products.

Vegetables

Fresh, home grown vegetables is a constant in-demand product. You can often beat the large supermarket chain on prices, and always on product quality. You can even become a supplier to small grocery stores. But most of your profits will come from direct retail sales to consumers who are looking for 'farm fresh, chemical free' produce. There are literally dozens of different vegetable crops you can grow. I recommend that you pick 8 or 10 of the most popular vegetables. Using intensive gardening techniques can greatly increase the amount produced per acre. Some growers have reported incomes of up to $20,000 per acre!

These are a few of the most popular vegetables: Asparagus — yields up to 2,000 pounds per acre at $2 per pound. Plants are started as roots and are ready to use in about 3 years. And will continue producing for up to 20 years. Beans — always one of the most popular crops; and come in many easy-to-grow varieties. Beans will produce several crops each growing season. Brussels Sprouts — relatively easy to grow and can produce late into the year, even after a frost. Carrots — requires lots of loose fertile soil. There is a strong demand for 'baby carrots'. Corn — one of the most popular fresh picked vegetables, although it does have a slightly lower profitability per acre.

Lettuce — a quick and easy-to-grow vegetable. You should grow several different varieties, and it can be planted very early. Peppers — both the mild and hot varieties. Peppers need a long warm growing season and well drained soil. Other popular items include okra, onions, peas, radishes, spinach, squash, tomatoes, watermelon, and egg plant. Vegetables can be marketed in a variety of ways. There are even many 'U-Pick' vegetable operations. However, by far the best way to sell vegetables is by operating a small roadside stand, or at an established farmer's market. Most communities have a farmer's market operating on weekends. There's a booming market for organically grown vegetables. And that market will continue. Chemical free produce will always bring you premium prices. Organically grown vegetables take a little more soil preparation and effort, but they can be well worth the extra effort. Other ways to market vegetables are: directly to restaurants, local stores, and to food co-ops. The key to all of these marketing efforts is to have a high quality, chemical free products.

Speciality Crops

This section will briefly cover other special cash crops. Some of these crops can only be grown in certain section of the countries. Also, some must have special growing conditions.

Landscaping Plants

Special plants for landscaping are always in demand. These plants include shrubs such as: rhododendron, azaleas and juniper, as well as some decorative trees. Landscaping plants can be sold directly to the consumer or to landscaping companies. If you begin supplying a landscape company or retail outlets with good stock, you'll soon have a steady source of income. A couple of important things to know about landscape plants are that they must be attractive and have a good survival rate. And you probably need to give some sort of guarantee that the plants are free from disease.

Nut Crops

Including almonds, chestnuts, filberts, pecans and walnuts. You can expect a wait of from 3 to 20 years for nut production. But some growers also produce and sell various aged nut trees for replanting. Nice two and three old trees will bring a premium price. Since nut tree crops require a long time to mature, some growers use a dual method ... they plant a raspberry crop between the nut trees. It takes about 8 to 10 years to get nut trees into nut production. But, after they have produced crops, they can also be used for valuable lumber production in 30 years or so. Nut trees could make an excellent retirement crop if you plant them while you're young. Some arrow-straight walnut trees, black walnut specifically, have brought as much as $10,000 each!

Bamboo

This crop is grown for its edible shoots, and can produce 3 to 10 tons per acre. Bamboo is also used for a wide variety of construction items, including furniture. Currently, U.S. growers cannot keep up with the demand, so bamboo is being imported from Asia.

Dried Plants

Dried Plants are used for decoration and fragrance. Dried floral arrangements are especially popular. Many arts and craft shops, gift stores and specialty shops need a constant supply of dried flowers. There are two steps involved in producing these crops. First you must produce an attractive, quality plant. Next, you must use the proper drying techniques to preserve the plants while maintaining its looks.

Mushrooms

Mushrooms have become a very popular specialty food in fancy restaurants. The Shitake mushroom is specially adapted for production by small family farms. It can be harvested during the spring and fall. And it has both a meaty taste and medicinal properties. These mushrooms are usually grown outdoors on 6 to 8 foot logs. The logs are prepared and then inoculated with the mushroom spores. Then it's a 6 to 8 month wait for the first crop. Recently, a few growers have developed indoor growing techniques which result in a shorter growing season.

Oyster Mushrooms

It is another variety that is fast becoming popular. These mushrooms are fast growing and produce high yields. They can be grown on easily available material, such as wheat straw. The largest market for specialty mushrooms are restaurants, food co-ops, grocers and health food stores. You can enjoy a year round booming market for dried Shitake mushrooms.

Seeds

Many small growers are supplying the large seed companies with special crop seed. These include flower seeds, wildflowers seeds and hard-to-find vegetables. Some small producers occasionally sell directly to the consumer.

Sprouts

Sprouts growing sprouts can be ideal for those who have very little space. Fresh sprouts can be supplied to major grocery stores as well as to restaurants and health food stores.

Marketing Techniques

There are a variety of selling techniques that can be used get cash from your crops. Some producers use several of the methods at the same time. Several things can help make your marketing efforts easier. The first is quality. You want to produce the best product possible. Your product's good, clean, healthy appearance will impress buyers. Sub-par products will be hard to sell. The way to produce quality is by proper initial soil preparation, using good seeds and by adhering to accepted growing methods. You should read books about gardening and carefully study any special growing requirements for each vegetable or fruit. Books covering most all special plants and produce are available at your library or from the U.S. Government Printing Office in Washington DC. Also, you'll want to take steps to eliminate pests that injure your plants. There many plants that act as natural repellents to some insect pests. For example: basil, catnip, marigolds, nasturtiums, savory, garlic, horseradish, tansy, and thyme. An important marketing consideration is timing. If you can get a crop ready when other producers aren't, sales will be easy.

This can be done by using greenhouses, planting early, using hotbeds and, of course, good planning. Pricing is also important. Most sellers recommend that you price your products 10 per cent to 20 per cent below those in grocery stores. (But don't lock yourself into a price war by trying to undercut your competition from other small producers.) Products that are grown using organic methods will most often bring higher prices. Check will all the local retail stores and at farmers markets to get a feel for your local current selling rates. One of the most common marketing techniques is selling your wares at roadside stands. Two of the most important factors to consider before setting up your stand are signs and ample parking space. Your signs should be no longer than 6 to 8 words, neat, legible and easy to understand. Signs need to be placed far enough ahead of your stand to give the customer time to pull into your parking area. Next, you want your stand to be well organized and neat in appearance. Make it easy for the customer to see the product and prices. Neatness and cleanliness will pay off. Combined with quality products and good prices, you'll enjoy a lot of free advertising by 'word of mouth'. A variation of the roadside stand is to sell from the back of your pick-up truck or car. You'll need to locate a well travelled road and a spot with parking that doesn't interfere with anyone. Of course, all of the previously mentioned factors apply.

Another common selling method is at farmer's markets and flea markets. These gatherings are held in most localities. If not, you'll want to get together with other producers and organize a farmer's market. All of these methods can also be aided by advertising in local newspapers, 'penny saver' papers, radio stations, and by posting notices on bulletin boards. Selling directly to retail grocery stores and restaurants is another good procedure. If you can provide them with a steady supply of fresh produce, sales should be easy. When contacting these stores be prepared to offer a 30 per cent to 40 per cent discount from regular retail prices. This allows the retailer a good profit margin. If you are a reliable producer, you may be able to set up a weekly route to service several retail locations. There are many food co-ops that are eager to buy large quantities of quality produce. You'll need to offer reasonable discounts. Too, you'll want to scout out these local co-ops and contact them directly. For some products you may have to prepare neat individualized packages of produce. Example: 1 or 2 ounces of herbs in labelled, plastic bags. U-Pick operations have been discussed previously. This marketing method will work for almost any product. However, it does present some special problems. Example: you cannot let very young kids into the picking areas as they may get hurt and/or damage some crops. In order to operate a successful U-Pick operation, you'll need to get along well with people. You also need to be friendly, courteous and treat everyone as if they are individually important which, of course, they are.

There's a variety of ways to get help with gardening and marketing your products. Almost every state offers free agriculture help through universities and state agriculture offices. The U.S. Department of Agriculture also offers many free programmes. Local bookstores, newsstands, and libraries also contain many informative sources. Study these diligently and become skillful in gardening. Finally, you'll be able to find many newsletters and growers associations advertised in the gardening magazines. These are often your best sources for plants, seeds, growing techniques, and marketing strategies.

Success Analysis

Eight contributing factors are measured on a 1 to 10 basis (with ten being excellent) based on analysis of this opportunity.

1. Time Investment eight.
2. Start-up costs eight.
3. Gross income potential eight.
4. New income potential nine.
5. Income in relation to investment nine.
6. Stability seven.
7. Overall risk nine.
8. Potential for growth.
9. Overall Potential for Success eight.
10. This is basically a labour intensive business, relying on your learned skills and work.

Preparing the soil, planting, nurturing, harvesting and marketing are all details to which you must attend to on a continuous basis. Starting a backyard cash crop operation can be very, very rewarding. Plus, you'll not only get closer to nature while learning a valuable age-old skill, but you'll be producing a valuable, healthy product. 'Cash Crops' is an enjoyable business you can start with little money, nearly risk free. It can also give you wonderful personal satisfaction and, quite possibly, help to improve your health by working in the outdoors.

13 Climate

Climate encompasses the temperatures, humidity, atmospheric pressure, winds, rainfall, atmospheric particle count and numerous other meteorological elements in a given region over long periods of time, as opposed to the term weather, which refers to current activity of these same elements. The climate of a location is affected by its latitude, terrain, altitude, persistent ice or snow cover, as well as nearby oceans and their currents. Climates can be classified using parameters such as temperature and rainfall to define specific climate types. The most commonly used classification scheme is the one originally developed by Wladimir Köppen. The Thornthwaite system, in use since 1948, incorporates evapotranspiration in addition to temperature and precipitation information and is used in studying animal species diversity and potential impacts of climate changes. The Bergeron and Spatial Synoptic Classification systems focus on the origin of air masses defining the climate for certain areas.

Paleoclimatology is the study and description of ancient climates using information from both non-biotic factors such as sediments found in lake beds and ice cores, and biotic factors such as tree rings and coral, and can be used to extend back the temperature or rainfall information for particular locations to a time before various weather instruments were used to monitor weather conditions. Climate models are mathematical models of past, present and future climates and can be used to describe the likely patterns of future changes.

Climate (from Ancient Greek *klima*, meaning *inclination*) is commonly defined as the weather averaged over a long period of time. The standard averaging period is 30 years, but other periods may be used depending on the purpose. Climate also includes statistics other than the average, such as the magnitudes of day-to-day or year-to-year variations. The Intergovernmental Panel on Climate Change (IPCC) glossary definition is:

> Climate in a narrow sense is usually defined as the 'average weather', or more rigorously, as the statistical description in terms of the mean and variability of relevant quantities over a period of time ranging from months to thousands or millions of years. The classical period is 30 years, as defined by the World Meteorological Organization (WMO). These quantities are most often surface variables such as temperature, precipitation, and wind. Climate in a wider sense is the state, including a statistical description, of the climate system.

The difference between climate and weather is usefully summarized by the popular phrase 'Climate is what you expect, weather is what you get'. Over historical time spans there are a number of static variables that determine climate, including latitude, altitude, proportion of land to water, and proximity to oceans and mountains. Other climate determinants are more dynamic: for example, the thermohaline circulation of the ocean leads to a 5 °C (9 °F) warming of the northern Atlantic ocean compared to other ocean basins. Other ocean currents redistribute heat between land and water on a more regional scale. The density and type of vegetation coverage affects solar heat absorption, water retention, and rainfall on a regional level. Alterations in the quantity of atmospheric greenhouse gases determines the amount of solar energy retained by the planet, leading to global warming or global cooling. The variables which determine climate are numerous and the interactions complex, but there is general agreement that the broad outlines are understood, at least insofar as the determinants of historical climate change are concerned.

Climate Classification

There are several ways to classify climates into similar regimes. Originally, climes were defined in Ancient Greece to describe the weather depending upon a location's latitude. Modern climate classification methods can be broadly divided into *genetic* methods, which focus on the causes of climate, and *empiric* methods, which focus on the effects of climate. Examples of genetic classification include methods based on the relative frequency of different air mass types or locations within synoptic weather disturbances. Examples of empiric classifications include climate zones defined by plant hardiness, evapotranspiration, air mass origin, or more generally the Köppen climate classification which was originally designed to identify the climates associated with certain biomes. A common shortcoming of these classification schemes is that they produce distinct boundaries between the zones they define, rather than the gradual transition of climate properties more common in nature.

Bergeron and Spatial Synoptic

The most generic classification is that involving the concept of air masses. The Bergeron classification is the most widely accepted form of air mass classification. Air mass classification involves three letters. The first letter describes its moisture properties, with *c* used for continental air masses (dry) and *m* for maritime air masses (moist). The second letter describes the thermal characteristic of its source region: *T* for tropical, *P* for polar, *A* for Arctic or Antarctic,

M for monsoon, *E* for equatorial, and *S* for superior air (dry air formed by significant downward motion in the atmosphere). The third letter is used to designate the stability of the atmosphere. If the air mass is colder than the ground below it, it is labelled *k*. If the air mass is warmer than the ground below it, it is labelled *w*. While air mass identification was originally used in weather forecasting during the 1950s, climatologists began to establish synoptic climatologies based on this idea in 1973.

Based upon the Bergeron classification scheme is the Spatial Synoptic Classification system (SSC). There are six categories within the SSC scheme: Dry Polar (similar to continental polar), Dry Moderate (similar to maritime superior), Dry Tropical (similar to continental tropical), Moist Polar (similar to maritime polar), Moist Moderate (a hybrid between maritime polar and maritime tropical), and Moist Tropical (similar to maritime tropical, maritime monsoon, or maritime equatorial).

Köppen

Monthly average surface temperatures from 1961-1990. This is an example of how climate varies with location and season.

The Köppen classification includes climate regimes such as rain forest, monsoon, tropical savanna, humid subtropical, humid continental, oceanic climate, Mediterranean climate, steppe, subarctic climate, tundra, polar ice cap, and desert.

Rain forests are characterized by high rainfall, with definitions setting minimum normal annual rainfall between 1,750 millimetres (69 in) and 2,000 millimetres (79 in). Mean monthly temperatures exceed 18°C (64°F) during all months of the year.

A monsoon is a seasonal prevailing wind which lasts for several months, ushering in a region's rainy season.

Regions such as within North America, South America. Sub-Saharan Africa, Australia and East Asia to qualify as monsoon regimes.

A tropical savanna is a grassland biome located in semi-arid to semi-humid climate regions of subtropical and tropical latitudes, with average temperatures remain at or above 18°C (64°F) year round and rainfall between 750 millimetres (30 in) and 1,270 millimetres (50 in) a year. They are widespread on Africa, and are also found in India, the northern parts of South America, Malaysia, and Australia.

The humid subtropical climate zone where winter rainfall (and sometimes snowfall) is associated with large storms that the westerlies steer from west to east. Most summer rainfall occurs during thunderstorms and from occasional tropical cyclones. Humid subtropical climates lie on the east side continents, roughly between latitudes 20° and 40° away from the equator.

A humid continental climate is marked by variable weather patterns and a large seasonal temperature variance. Places with a hottest monthly temperature above 10 °C (50°F) and a coldest month temperature below -3°C (26.6°F) and which do not meet the criteria for an arid climate, are classified as continental.

An oceanic climate is typically found along the west coasts at the middle latitudes of all the world's continents, and in southeastern Australia, and is accompanied by plentiful precipitation year round.

The Mediterranean climate regime resembles the climate of the lands in the Mediterranean Basin, parts of western North America, parts of Western and South Australia, in southwestern South Africa and in parts of central Chile. The climate is characterized by hot, dry summers and cool, wet winters.

A steppe is a dry grassland with an annual temperature range in the summer of up to 40 °C (104 °F) and during the winter down to -40°C (-40°F).

A subarctic climate has little precipitation and monthly temperatures which are above 10 °C (50 °F) for one to three months of the year, with continuous permafrost due to the very cold winters. Winters within subarctic climates include up to six months of temperatures averaging below 0°C (32°F).

Tundra occurs in the far Northern Hemisphere, north of the Taiga belt, including vast areas of northern Russia and Canada

A polar ice cap, or polar ice sheet, is a high-latitude region of a planet or moon that is covered in ice. Ice caps form because high-latitude regions receive less energy in the form of solar radiation from the sun than equatorial regions, resulting in lower surface temperatures.

A desert is a landscape form or region that receives very little precipitation. Deserts usually have a large diurnal and seasonal temperature range, with high daytime temperatures (in summer up to 45°C or 113°F), and low night-time temperatures (in winter down to 0°C; 32°F) due to extremely low humidity. Many deserts are formed by rain shadows, as mountains block the path of moisture and precipitation to the desert.

This climate classification method monitors the soil water budget using the concept of evapotranspiration. It monitors the portion of total precipitation used to nourish vegetation over a certain area. It uses indices such as a humidity index and an aridity index to determine an area's moisture regime based upon its average temperature, average rainfall, and average vegetation type. The lower the value of the index is any given area, the drier the area is.

The moisture classification includes climatic classes with descriptors such as hyperhumid, humid, subhumid, subarid, semi-arid (values of -20 to -40), and arid (values below 40). Humid regions experience more precipitation than evaporation each year, while arid regions experience greater evaporation than precipitation on an annual basis. A total of 33 per cent of the earth's landmass is considered either arid of semi-arid, including southwest North America, southwest South America, most of northern and a small part of southern Africa, southwest and portions of eastern Asia, as well as much of Australia. Studies suggest that precipitation effectiveness (PE) within the Thornthwaite moisture index is overestimated in the summer and underestimated in the winter. This index can be effectively used to determine the number of herbivore and mammal species numbers within a given area. The index is also used in studies of climate change.

Thermal classifications within the Thornthwaite scheme include microthermal, mesothermal, and megathermal regimes. A mircothermal climate is one of low annual mean temperatures, generally between 0°C (32°F) and 14°C (57°F) which experiences short summers and has a potential evaporation between 14 centimetres (5.5 in) and 43 centimetres (17 in). A mesothermal climate lacks persistent heat or persistent cold, with potential evaporation between 57 centimetres (22 in) and 114 centimetres (45 in). A megathermal climate is one with persistent high temperatures and abundant rainfall, with potential evaporation in excess of 114 centimetres (45 in). Details of the modern climate record are known through the taking of measurements from such weather instruments as thermometers, barometers, and anemometers during the past few centuries. The instruments used to study weather conditions over the modern time scale, their known error, their immediate environment, and their exposure have changed over the years, which must be considered when studying the climate of centuries past.

Paleoclimatology

Paleoclimatology is the study of past climate over a great period of the Earth's history. It uses evidence from ice sheets, tree rings, sediments, coral, and rocks to determine the past state of the climate. It demonstrates periods of stability and periods of change and can indicate whether changes follow patterns such as regular cycles.

Climate Change

Variations in CO_2, temperature and dust from the Vostok ice core over the past 450,000 years Climate change refers to the variation in the Earth's global climate or in regional climates over time. It describes changes in the variability or average state of the atmosphere over time scales ranging from decades to millions of years. These changes can be caused by processes internal to the Earth, external forces (e.g. variations in sunlight intensity) or, more recently, human activities.

Earth has undergone periodic climate shifts in the past, including four major ice ages. These consisting of glacial periods where conditions are colder than normal, separated by interglacial periods. The accumulation of snow and ice during a glacial period increases the surface albedo, reflecting more of the Sun's energy into space and maintaining a lower atmospheric temperature. Increases in greenhouse gases, such as by volcanic activity, can increase the global temperature and produce an interglacial. Suggested causes of ice age periods include the positions of the continents, variations in the Earth's orbit, changes in the solar output, and vulcanism.

Climate Models

Climate models use quantitative methods to simulate the interactions of the atmosphere, oceans, land surface and ice. They are used for a variety of purposes from study of the dynamics of the weather and climate system to projections of future climate. All climate models balance, or very nearly balance, incoming energy as short wave (including visible) electromagnetic radiation to the earth with outgoing energy as long wave (infrared) electromagnetic radiation from the earth. Any imbalance results in a change in the average temperature of the earth.

The most talked-about models of recent years have been those relating temperature to the build-up of greenhouse gases in the atmosphere, primarily carbon dioxide (see greenhouse gas). These models predict an upward trend in the global mean surface temperature, with the most rapid increase in temperature being projected for the higher latitudes of the Northern Hemisphere.

Models can range from relatively simple to quite complex:

- A simple radiant heat transfer model that treats the earth as a single point and averages outgoing energy
- this can be expanded vertically (radiative-convective models), or horizontally
- finally, (coupled) atmosphere–ocean–global climate models discretise and solve the full equations for mass and energy transfer and radiant exchange.

14 Banana

Banana is the common name for a fruit and also the herbaceous plants of the genus *Musa* which produce this commonly eaten fruit. They are native to the tropical region of Southeast Asia. Bananas are likely to have been first domesticated in Papua New Guinea. Today, they are cultivated throughout the tropics.

Banana plants are of the family Musaceae. They are cultivated primarily for their fruit, and to a lesser extent for the production of fibre and as ornamental plants. As the banana plants are normally tall and fairly sturdy they are often mistaken for trees, but their main or upright stem is actually a *pseudostem* (literally 'fake stem'). For some species this pseudostem can reach a height of up to 2-8 m, with leaves of up to 3.5 m in length. Each pseudostem can produce a bunch of yellow, green or even red bananas before dying and being replaced by another pseudostem.

The banana fruit grow in hanging clusters, with up to 20 fruit to a tier (called a *hand*), and 3-20 tiers to a bunch. The total of the hanging clusters is known as a bunch, or commercially as a 'banana stem', and can weigh from 30-50 kg. The fruit averages 125 g, of which approximately 75 per cent is water and 25 per cent dry matter content. Each individual fruit (known as a banana or 'finger') has a protective outer layer (a peel or skin) with a fleshy edible inner portion. Both skin and inner part can be eaten raw or cooked. Western cultures generally eat the inside raw and throw away the skin while some Asian cultures generally eat both the skin and inside cooked. Typically, the fruit has numerous strings (called 'phloem bundles') which run between the skin and inner part. Bananas are a valuable source of vitamin B_6, vitamin C, and potassium.

Bananas are grown in at least 107 countries. In popular culture and commerce, 'banana' usually refers to soft, sweet 'dessert' bananas. The bananas from a group of cultivars with firmer, starchier fruit are called plantains. Bananas may also be cut and dried and eaten as a type of chip. Dried bananas are also ground into banana flour.

Although the wild species have fruits with numerous large, hard seeds, virtually all culinary bananas have seedless fruits. Bananas are classified either as dessert bananas (meaning they are yellow and fully ripe when eaten) or as green cooking bananas. Almost all export bananas are of the dessert types; however, only about 10-15 per cent of all production is for export, with the United States and European Union being the dominant buyers.

The banana plant is a pseudostem that grows to 6 to 7.6 metres (20-25 feet) tall, growing from a corm. Leaves are spirally arranged and may grow 2.7 metres (9 ft) long and 60 cm (2 ft) wide. The banana plant is the largest of all herbaceous flowering plants. The large leaves grow whole, but are easily torn by the wind, resulting in the familiar frond look.

A single, sterile, male banana flower, also known as the *banana heart* is normally produced by each stem (though on rare occasions more can be produced — a single plant in the Philippines has five. Banana hearts are used as a vegetable in Southeast Asia, steamed, in salads, or eaten raw. The female flowers are produced further up the stem and produce the actual fruit without requiring fertilization. The fruit has been described as a 'leathery berry'. In cultivated varieties, the seeds have degenerated nearly to non-existence; their remnants are tiny black specks in the interior of the fruit. The ovary is inferior to the flower; because of their stiff stems and the positioning of the ovary and flower, bananas grow sticking up, not hanging down.

Some sources assert that the genus of the banana, *Musa*, is named for Antonio Musa, physician to the Emperor Augustus. Others say that Linnaeus, who gave the genus its name in 1750, simply adapted an Arabic word for banana, *mauz*. The word *banana* itself comes from the Arabic word *banan*, which means 'finger'. The genus contains numerous species; several produce edible fruit, while others are cultivated as ornamentals.

Bananas come in a variety of sizes and colours when ripe, including yellow, purple, and red. Bananas can be eaten raw though some varieties are generally cooked first. Depending upon cultivar and ripeness, the flesh can vary in taste from starchy to sweet, and texture from firm to mushy. Unripe or green bananas and plantains are used for cooking various dishes such as banana pudding and are the staple starch of many tropical populations. Banana sap is extremely sticky and can be used as a practical adhesive. Sap can be obtained from the pseudostem, from the fruit peelings, or from the fruit flesh.

Most production for local sale is of green cooking bananas and plantains, as ripe dessert bananas are easily damaged while being transported to market. Even when transported only within their country of origin, ripe bananas suffer a high rate of damage and loss.

The commercial dessert cultivars most commonly eaten in temperate countries (species *Musa acuminata* or the hybrid *Musa × paradisiaca*, a cultigen) are imported in large quantities from the tropics. They are popular in part because, being a non-seasonal crop, they are available fresh year-round. In global commerce, by far the most important of these banana cultivars is 'Cavendish', which accounts for the vast bulk of bananas exported from the tropics. The Cavendish gained popularity in the 1950s after the previously mass produced cultivar, Gros Michel, became commercially unviable due to Panama disease, a fungus which attacks the roots of the banana plant.

The most important properties making 'Cavendish' the main export banana are related to transport and shelf life rather than taste; major commercial cultivars rarely have a superior flavour compared to the less widespread cultivars. Export bananas are picked green, and then usually ripened in ripening rooms when they arrive in their country of destination. These are special rooms made air-tight and filled with ethylene gas to induce ripening. Bananas can be ordered by the retailer 'ungassed', however, and may show up at the supermarket still fully green. While these bananas will ripen more slowly, the flavor will be notably richer , and the banana peel can be allowed to reach a yellow/brown speckled phase, and yet retain a firm flesh inside. Thus, shelf life is somewhat extended.

The vivid yellow colour normally associated with supermarket bananas is in fact a side-effect of the artificial ripening process. Cavendish bananas that have been allowed to ripen naturally on the plant have a greenish-yellow appearance which changes to a brownish-yellow as they ripen further. Although both the flavour and texture of 'tree ripened' bananas is generally regarded as superior to any type green-picked fruit, once natural ripening has commenced the shelf life is typically only 7-10 days, making commercial distribution impractical. For most people the only practical means of obtaining such fruit is growing it themselves, however this is also somewhat problematic, as the bananas all tend to ripen at once and have very poor keeping properties.

The flavour and texture of bananas are also affected by the temperature at which they ripen. Bananas are refrigerated to between 13.5 and 15°C (57 and 59°F) during transportation. At lower temperatures, the ripening of bananas permanently stalls, and the bananas will eventually turn gray as cell walls break down. The skins of ripe bananas will quickly turn black in the 4°C environment of a domestic refrigerator, although the fruit inside remains unaffected.

It should be noted that *Musa paradisiaca* is also the generic name for the common plantain, a coarser and starchier variant not to be confused with *Musa acuminata* or the Cavendish variety.

In addition to the fruit, the flower of the banana plant (also known as *banana blossom* or *banana heart*) is used in Southeast Asian, Tamil, Bengali, and Kerala (India) cuisine, either served raw with dips or cooked in soups and curries. The tender core of the banana plant's trunk is also used in Bengali and Kerala cooking, and notably in the Burmese dish mohinga. Bananas fried with batter is a popular dessert in Malaysia, Singapore, and Indonesia. Banana fritters can be served with ice cream as well. Bananas are also eaten deep fried, baked in their skin in a split bamboo, or steamed in glutinous rice wrapped in a banana leaf in Burma where bunches of green bananas surrounding a green coconut in a tray form an important part of traditional offerings to the Buddha and the Nats. The juice extract prepared from the tender core is used to treat kidney stones.

The leaves of the banana plant are large, flexible, and waterproof. They are used many ways, including as umbrellas and to wrap food for cooking or storage. Banana leaves are also used to serve food in India and other Asian countries.

Banana chips are a snack produced from dehydrated or fried banana or plantain slices, which have a dark brown colour and an intense banana taste. Bananas have also been used in the making of jam. Unlike other fruits, it is difficult to extract juice from bananas because when compressed a banana simply turns to pulp.

Seeded bananas (*Musa balbisiana*), the forerunner of the common domesticated banana, are sold in markets in Indonesia.

In India, juice is extracted from the corm and used as a home remedy for the treatment of jaundice, sometimes with the addition of honey.

Bananas and plantains constitute a major staple food crop for millions of people in developing countries. In most tropical countries, green (unripe) bananas used for cooking represent the main cultivars. Cooking bananas are very similar to potatoes in how they are used. Both can be fried, boiled, baked, or chipped and have similar taste and texture when served. One green cooking banana has about the same calorie content as one potato.

In 2003, India led the world in banana production, representing approximately 23 per cent of the worldwide crop, most of which was for domestic consumption. The four leading banana exporting countries were Ecuador, Costa Rica, the Philippines, and Colombia, which together accounted for about two-thirds of the world's exports, each exporting more than 1 million tons. Ecuador alone provided more than 30 per cent of global banana exports, according to FAO statistics.

The vast majority of producers are small-scale farmers growing the crop either for home consumption or for local markets. Because bananas and plantains will produce fruit year-round, they provide an extremely valuable source of food during the hunger season (that period of time when all the food from the previous harvest has been consumed, and the next harvest is still some time away). It is for these reasons that bananas and plantains are of major importance to food security.

Bananas are among the most widely consumed foods in the world. Most banana farmers receive a low unit price for their produce as supermarkets buy enormous supermarkets has led to reduced margins in recent years which in turn has led to lower prices for growers. Chiquita, Del Monte, Dole, and Fyffes grow their own bananas in Ecuador, Colombia, Costa Rica, Guatemala, and Honduras. Banana plantations are capital intensive and demand high expertise, so the majority of independent growers are large and wealthy landowners of these countries. This has led to bananas being available as a 'fair trade' or Rainforest Alliance certified item in some countries.

The banana has an extensive trade history beginning with the founding of the United Fruit Company (now Chiquita) at the end of the nineteenth century. For much of the 20th century, bananas and coffee dominated the export economies of Central America. In the 1930s, bananas and coffee made up as much as 75 per cent of the region's exports. As late as 1960, the two crops accounted for 67 per cent of the exports from the region. Though the two were grown in similar regions, they tended not to be distributed together. The United Fruit Company based its business almost entirely on the banana trade, as the coffee trade proved too difficult for it to control. The term 'banana republic' has been broadly applied to most countries in Central America, but from a strict economic perspective only Costa Rica, Honduras, and Panama were actual 'banana republics', countries with economies dominated by the banana trade.

The countries of the European Union have traditionally imported many of their bananas from the former European island colonies of the Caribbean, paying guaranteed prices above global market rates. As of 2005, these arrangements were in the process of being withdrawn under pressure from other major trading powers, principally the United States. The withdrawal of these indirect subsidies to Caribbean producers is expected to favour the banana producers of Central America, in which American companies have an economic interest.

The United States has minimal banana production. 14,000 tons of bananas were grown in Hawaii in 2001. Bananas have also been grown in Florida and southern California.

The domestication of bananas took place in southeastern Asia. Many species of wild bananas still exist in New Guinea, Malaysia, Indonesia, and the Philippines. Recent archaeological and palaeoenvironmental evidence at Kuk Swamp in the Western Highlands Province of Papua New Guinea suggests that banana cultivation there goes back to at least 5000 BCE, and possibly to 8000 BCE. This would make the New Guinean highlands the place where bananas were first domesticated. It is likely that other species of wild bananas were later also domesticated elsewhere in southeastern Asia. Southeast Asia is the region of primary diversity of the banana. Areas of secondary diversity are found in Africa, indicating a long history of banana cultivation in the region.

Actual and probable diffusion of bananas during Islamic times (700-1500 AD).

Some recent discoveries of banana phytoliths in Cameroon dating to the first millennium BCE have triggered an as yet unresolved debate about the antiquity of banana cultivation in Africa. There is linguistic evidence that bananas were already known in Madagascar around that time. The earliest evidence of banana cultivation in Africa before these recent discoveries dates to no earlier than late 6th century AD. In this view, bananas were introduced to the east coast of Africa by Muslim Arabs.

The banana may have been present in isolated locations of the Middle East on the eve of the rise of Islam. There is some textual evidence that the prophet Muhammad was familiar with it. The spread of Islam was followed by the far reaching diffusion of bananas. There are numerous references to it in Islamic texts (such as poems and hadiths) beginning in the ninth century. By the tenth century the banana appears in texts from Palestine and Egypt. From there it diffused into north Africa and Muslim Spain. In fact, during the mediaeval ages, bananas from Granada were considered amongst the best in the Arab world. In 650, Islamic conquerors brought the banana to Palestine.

Bananas were introduced to the Americas by Portuguese sailors who brought the fruits from West Africa in the 1500s. The word banana is of West African origin, and passed into English via Spanish or Portuguese.

In the 15th and 16th century, Portuguese colonists started banana plantations in the Atlantic Islands, Brazil, and western Africa. As late as the Victorian Era, bananas were not widely known in Europe, although they were available via merchant trade. Jules Verne references bananas with detailed descriptions so as not to confuse readers in his book *Around the World in Eighty Days* (1872).

In the early 20th century, bananas began forming the basis of large commercial empires, exemplarized by the United Fruit Company, which created immense banana plantations especially in Central and South America. These were usually extremely commercially exploitative, and the term 'Banana republic' was coined for states like Honduras and Guatemala, representing the fact that 'servile dictatorships' were created and abetted by these companies and their political backers, for example in the USA.

While the original bananas contained rather large seeds, triploid (and thus seedless) cultivars have been selected for human consumption. These are propagated asexually from offshoots of the plant. The plant is allowed to produce 2 shoots at a time; a larger one for fruiting immediately and a smaller 'sucker' or 'follower' that will produce fruit in 6-8 months time. The life of a banana plantation is 25 years or longer, during which time the individual stools or planting sites may move slightly from their original positions as lateral rhizome formation dictates.

Cultivated bananas are *parthenocarpic*, which makes them sterile and unable to produce viable seeds. Lacking seeds, another form of propagation is required. This normally involves removing and transplanting part of the underground stem (called a corm). Usually this is done by carefully removing a sucker (a vertical shoot that develops from the base of the banana pseudostem) with some roots intact. However, small sympodial corms, representing not yet elongated suckers, are easier to transplant and can be left out of the ground for up to 2 weeks; they require minimal care and can be boxed together for shipment.

Contrary to what is widely believed, it is not actually necessary to include any of the corm or root structure to propagate bananas; severed suckers with no root material attached can be successfully propagated in damp sand, although this takes somewhat longer.

In some countries, bananas are also commercially propagated by means of tissue culture. This method is preferred since it ensures disease-free planting material. When using vegetative parts such as suckers for propagation, there is a risk of transmitting diseases (especially the devastating Panama disease).

Pests, Diseases, and Natural Disasters

While in no danger of outright extinction, the most common edible banana cultivar 'Cavendish' (extremely popular in Europe and the Americas) could become unviable for large-scale cultivation in the next 10-20 years. Its predecessor 'Gros Michel', discovered in the 1820s, has already suffered this fate. Like almost all bananas, it lacks genetic diversity, which makes it vulnerable to diseases, which threaten both commercial cultivation and the small-scale subsistence farming. Some commentators have further remarked that those variants which could replace what much of the world considers a 'typical banana' are so different that most people would not consider them the same fruit, and blame the decline of the banana on monogenetic cultivation driven by short-term commercial exploitation motives.

Panama Disease (Race 1) — fusarium wilt (a soil fungus). The fungus enters the plants through the roots and moves up with water into the trunk and leaves, producing gels and gums. These plug and cut off the flow of water and nutrients, causing the plant to wilt. Prior to 1960 almost all commercial banana production centered on the cultivar ' Gros Michel', which was highly susceptible to fusarium wilt and collapse, exposing the rest of the plant to lethal amounts of sunlight . The cultivar 'Cavendish' was chosen as a replacement for 'Gros Michel' because out of the resistant cultivars it was viewed as producing the highest quality fruit. However, more care is required for shipping the 'Cavendish' banana, and its quality compared to 'Gros Michel' is debated.

However, according to current references, a deadly form of Panama disease is infecting the world's Cavendish banana plants. All are genetically identical, which causes problems when it comes to disease resistance.

Tropical Race 4 — a reinvigorated strain of Panama disease first discovered in 1993. This is a virulent form of fusarium wilt that has wiped out 'Cavendish' in several southeast Asian countries. It has yet to reach the Americas; however, soil fungi can easily be carried on boots clothing, or tools. This is how Tropical Race 4 moves from one plantation to another and is its most likely route into Latin America. The Cavendish cultivar is highly susceptible to TR4, and over time, Cavendish is almost certain to be eliminated from commercial production by this disease. Unfortunately, the only known defense to TR4 is genetic resistance.

Black Sigatoka — a fungal leaf spot disease first observed in Fiji in 1963 or 1964. Black Sigatoka (also known as Black Leaf Streak) has spread to banana plantations throughout the tropics due to infected banana leaves being used as packing material. It affects all of the main cultivars of bananas and plantains, impeding photosynthesis by turning parts of their leaves black, and eventually killing the entire leaf. Being starved for energy, fruit production falls by 50 per cent or more, and the bananas that do grow suffer premature ripening, making them unsuitable for export. The fungus has shown ever increasing resistance to fungicidal treatment, with the current expense for treating one hectare exceeding $1000 per year. In addition to the financial expense there is the question of how long such intensive spraying can be justified environmentally. Several resistant cultivars of banana have been developed, but none has yet received wide scale commercial acceptance due to taste and texture issues.

Banana Bunchy Top Virus (BBTV) — this virus is spread from plant to plant by aphids. It causes stunting of the leaves resulting in a 'bunched' appearance. Generally, a banana plant infected with the virus will not set fruit, although mild strains exist in many areas which do allow for some fruit production. These mild strains are often mistaken for malnourishment, or a disease other than BBTV. There is no cure for BBTV, however its effect can be minimised by planting only tissue cultured plants (*In vitro* propagation), controlling the aphids, and immediately removing and destroying any plant from the field that shows signs of the disease.

Even though it is no longer viable for large scale cultivation, 'Gros Michel' is not extinct and is still grown in areas where Panama disease is not found. Likewise, 'Cavendish' is in no danger of extinction, but it may leave the shelves of the supermarkets for good if diseases make it impossible to supply the global market. It is unclear if any existing cultivar can replace 'Cavendish' on a scale needed to fill current demand, so various hybridisation and genetic engineering programmes are working on creating a disease-resistant, mass-market banana.

Australia

Australia is relatively free of plant diseases and therefore prohibits imports. When Cyclone Larry wiped out Australia's domestic banana crop in 2006, bananas became relatively expensive, due to both low supply domestically and the existence of laws prohibiting banana imports. Prices have since fallen as production has reverted back to a steady rate.

In East Africa

Most bananas grown worldwide are used for local consumption. In the tropics, bananas, especially cooking bananas, represent a major source of food, as well as a major source of income for smallholder farmers. It is in the East African highlands that bananas reach their greatest importance as a staple food crop. In countries such as Uganda, Burundi, and Rwanda per capita consumption has been estimated at 450 kg per year, the highest in the world. Ugandans use the same word 'matooke' to describe both banana and food.

In the past, the banana was a highly sustainable crop with a long plantation life and stable yields year round. However with the arrival of the Black sigatoka fungus, banana production in eastern Africa has fallen by over 40 per cent. For example, during the 1970s, Uganda produced 15 to 20 tonnes of bananas per hectare. Today, production has fallen to only 6 tonnes per hectare.

The situation has started to improve as new disease resistant cultivars have been developed by the International Institute of Tropical Agriculture and NARO such as the FHIA-17 (known in Uganda as the Kabana 3). These new cultivars taste different from the traditionally grown banana which has slowed their acceptance by local farmers. However, by adding mulch and animal manure to the soil around the base of the banana plant, these new cultivars have substantially increased yields in the areas where they have been tried.

The International Institute of Tropical Agriculture and NARO, funded by the Rockefeller Foundation and CGIAR have started trials for genetically modified banana plants that are resistant to both Black sigatoka and banana weevils. It is developing cultivars specifically for smallholder or subsistence farmers.

Allergic Reactions

There are two forms of banana allergy. One is oral allergy syndrome which causes itching and swelling in the mouth or throat within one hour after ingestion and is related to birch tree and other pollen allergies. The other is related to latex allergies and causes urticaria and potentially serious upper gastrointestinal symptoms.

The banana plant has long been a source of fibre for high quality textiles. In Japan, the cultivation of banana for clothing and household use dates back to at least the 13th century. In the Japanese system, leaves and shoots are cut from the plant periodically to ensure softness. The harvested shoots must first be boiled in lye to prepare the fibres for the making of the yarn. These banana shoots produce fibres of varying degrees of softness, yielding yarns and textiles with differing qualities for specific uses. For example, the outermost fibres of the shoots are the coarsest, and are suitable for tablecloths, whereas the softest innermost fibres are desirable for kimono and kamishimo. This traditional Japanese banana cloth making process requires many steps, all performed by hand.

In another system employed in Nepal, the trunk of the banana plant is harvested instead, small pieces of which are subjected to a softening process, mechanical extraction of the fibres, bleaching, and drying. After that, the fibres are sent to the Kathmandu Valley for the making of high end rugs with a textural quality similar to silk. These banana fibre rugs are woven by the traditional Nepalese hand-knotted methods, and are sold RugMark certified.

Paper

Banana fibre is also used in the production of banana paper. Banana paper is used in two different senses: to refer to a paper made from the bark of the banana plant, mainly used for artistic purposes, or paper made from banana fiber, obtained from an industrialized process, from the stem and the non-usable fruits. This paper can be either hand-made or made by industrialized machine.

Storage and Transport

In the current world marketing system, bananas are grown in the tropics. The fruit therefore has to be transported over long distances and storage is necessary. To gain maximum life, bunches are harvested before the fruit is fully mature. The fruit is carefully handled, transported quickly to the seaboard, cooled, and shipped under sophisticated refrigeration. The basis of this procedure is to prevent the bananas producing ethylene which is the natural ripening agent of the fruit. This sophisticated technology allows storage and transport for 3-4 weeks at 13 degrees Celsius. On arrival at the destination, the bananas are held at about 17 degrees Celsius and treated with a low concentration of ethylene. After a few days, the fruit has begun to ripen and it is distributed for retail sale. It is important to note that unripe bananas can not be held in the home refrigerator as they suffer from the cold. After ripening some bananas can be held for a few days at home. They can be stored indefinitely frozen, then eaten like an ice pop or cooked as a banana mush.

Recent studies have suggested that the presence of carbon dioxide (which is produced by the fruit) extends the life and the addition of an ethylene absorbent further extends the life even at high temperatures. This effect can be exploited by packing the fruit in a polyethylene bag and including an ethylene absorbent, potassium permanganate, on an inert carrier. The bag is then sealed with a band or string. This treatment has been shown to more than double the life of the bananas at a range of temperatures and can give a life of up to 3-4 weeks without the need for refrigeration.

The depiction of a person slipping on a banana peel has been a staple of physical comedy for generations. A 1906 comedy record produced by Edison Records features a popular character of the time, 'Cal Stewart', claiming to describe his own such incident, saying:

> I don't think much of a man what throws a bananer peelin' on the sidewalk, and I don't think much of a bananer what throws a man on the sidewalk, neither. ... my foot hit that bananer peelin' and I went up in the air, and come down ker-plunk, and fer about a minnit I seen all the stars what 'stronomy tells about, and some that hain't been discovered yit. Wall jist as I was pickin' myself up, a little boy come runnin' cross the street and he said, 'Oh mister, won't you please do that agin? My mother didn't see you do it'.

Arts

The poet Basho is named after the Japanese word for a banana plant. The 'basho' planted in his garden by a grateful student became a source of inspiration to his poetry, as well as a symbol of his life and home.

The song Yes! We Have No Bananas was written by Frank Silver and Irving Cohn and originally released in 1923; for many decades, it was the best-selling sheet music in history. Since then the song has been rerecorded several times and has been particularly popular during banana shortages.

Symbols

Bananas are also humourously used as a phallic symbol due to similarities in size and shape. This is typified by the artwork of the debut album of The Velvet Underground, which features a banana on the front cover, yet on the original LP version, the design allowed the listener to 'peel' this banana to find a pink, phallic structure on the inside.

A publication in Angewandte Chemie by Moser et al. (2008) mentions a recent and surprising finding. Ripe bananas exhibit a blue fluorescence when exposed to ultraviolet (UV) light (Black light). This property has been overlooked for a long time. Green bananas do not show any sign of fluorescence. The cause is attributed by the authors to the degradation of chlorophyll giving rise to the accumulation of a fluorescent product in the skin of the fruit. The chlorophyll breakdown product is stabilized by a propionate ester group. Banana-tree leaves also fluoresce in the same way. A possible consequence in nature is that animals capable of seeing in the UV spectrum would also be able to more quickly detect the ripened fruits.

15 Black Pepper

Black pepper (*Piper nigrum*) is a flowering vine in the family Piperaceae, cultivated for its fruit, which is usually dried and used as a spice and seasoning. The fruit, known as a peppercorn when dried, is a small drupe five millimetres in diameter, dark red when fully mature, containing a single seed. Peppercorns, and the powdered pepper derived from grinding them, may be described as black pepper, white pepper, red/pink pepper, green pepper, and very often simply pepper. The terms *pink peppercorns*, *red pepper*, and *green pepper* are also used to describe the fruits of other, unrelated plants.

Black pepper is native to South India (Tamil: *milagu*; Kannada: *meNasu*; Malayalam: *kurumulaku*; Telugu: *miriyam*; Konkani: *miriya konu*;) and is extensively cultivated there and elsewhere in tropical regions. Black pepper is also cultivated in the Coorg area of Karnataka.

Dried ground pepper is one of the most common spices in European cuisine and its descendants, having been known and prized since antiquity for both its flavour and its use as a medicine. The spiciness of black pepper is due to the chemical piperine. It may be found on nearly every dinner table in some parts of the world, often alongside table salt.

The word 'pepper' is ultimately derived from the Sanskrit *pippali*, the word for long pepper via the Latin *piper* which was used by the Romans to refer both to pepper and long pepper, as the Romans erroneously believed that both of these spices were derived from the same plant. The English word for pepper is derived from the Old English *pipor*. The Latin word is also the source of German *Pfeffer*, French *poivre*, Dutch *peper*, and other similar forms. In the 16th century, *pepper* started referring to the unrelated New World chile peppers as well. 'Pepper' was used in a figurative sense to mean 'spirit' or 'energy' at least as far back as the 1840s; in the early 20th century, this was shortened to *pep*.

Black pepper is produced from the still-green unripe berries of the pepper plant. The berries are cooked briefly in hot water, both to clean them and to prepare them for drying. The heat ruptures cell walls in the fruit, speeding the work of browning enzymes during drying. The berries are dried in the sun or by machine for several days, during which the fruit around the seed shrinks and darkens into a thin, wrinkled black layer. Once dried, the fruits are called black peppercorns.

White pepper consists of the seed only, with the skin of the fruit removed. This is usually accomplished by process known as retting, where fully ripe berries are soaked in water for about a week, during which the flesh of the fruit softens and decomposes. Rubbing then removes what remains of the fruit, and the naked seed is dried. Alternative processes are used for removing the outer fruit from the seed, including decortication, the removal of the outer layer from black pepper from berries through mechanical, chemical or biological methods.

In the U.S., white pepper is often used in dishes like light-coloured sauces or mashed potatoes, where ground black pepper would visibly stand out. There is disagreement regarding which is generally spicier. They have differing flavours due to the presence of certain compounds in the outer fruit layer of the berry that are not found in the seed. *folius*), and white peppercorns.

Green pepper, like black, is made from the unripe berries. Dried green peppercorns are treated in a manner that retains the green colour, such as treatment with sulfur dioxide or freeze-drying. Pickled peppercorns, also green, are unripe berries preserved in brine or vinegar. Fresh, unpreserved green pepper berries, largely unknown in the West, are used in some Asian cuisines, particularly Thai cuisine. Their flavour has been described as piquant and fresh, with a bright aroma. They decay quickly if not dried or preserved.

A product called orange pepper or red pepper consists of ripe red pepper berries preserved in brine and vinegar. Ripe red peppercorns can also be dried using the same colour-preserving techniques used to produce green pepper Pink pepper from *Piper nigrum* is distinct from the more-common dried 'pink peppercorns', which are the fruits of a plant from a different family, the Peruvian pepper tree, *Schinus molle*, and its relative the Brazilian pepper tree, *Schinus terebinthifolius*. In years past there was debate as to the health safety of pink peppercorns, which is mostly no longer an issue. Sichuan peppercorn is another 'pepper' that is botanically unrelated to black pepper.

Peppercorns are often categorised under a label describing their region or port of origin. Two well-known types come from India's Malabar Coast: Malabar pepper and Tellicherry pepper. Tellicherry is a higher-grade pepper, made from the largest, ripest 10 per cent of berries from Malabar plants grown on Mount Tellicherry. Sarawak pepper is produced in the Malaysian portion of Borneo, and Lampong pepper on Indonesia's island of Sumatra. White Muntok pepper is another Indonesian product, from Bangka Island.

The pepper plant is a perennial woody vine growing to four metres in height on supporting trees, poles, or trellises. It is a spreading vine, rooting readily where trailing stems touch the ground. The leaves are alternate, entire, five to ten centimetres long and three to six centimetres broad. The flowers are small, produced on pendulous spikes four to eight centimetres long at the leaf nodes, the spikes lengthening to seven to 15 centimeters as the fruit matures. Black pepper is grown in soil that is neither too dry nor susceptible to flooding, moist, well-drained and rich in organic matter. The plants are propagated by cuttings about 40 to 50 centimetres long, tied up to neighbouring trees or climbing frames at distances of about two metres apart; trees with rough bark are favoured over those with smooth bark, as the pepper plants climb rough bark more readily. Competing plants are cleared away, leaving only sufficient trees to provide shade and permit free ventilation. The roots are covered in leaf mulch and manure, and the shoots are trimmed twice a year. On dry soils the young plants require watering every other day during the dry season for the first three years. The plants bear fruit from the fourth or fifth year, and typically continue to bear fruit for seven years. The cuttings are usually cultivars, selected both for yield and quality of fruit. A single stem will bear 20 to 30 fruiting spikes. The harvest begins as soon as one or two berries at the base of the spikes begin to turn red, and before the fruit is mature, but when full grown and still hard; if allowed to ripen, the berries lose pungency, and ultimately fall off and are lost. The spikes are collected and spread out to dry in the sun, then the peppercorns are stripped off the spikes.

Black pepper is native to India. Within the genus *Piper*, it is most closely related to other Asian species such as *Piper caninum*.

Pepper has been used as a spice in India since prehistoric times. Pepper is native to India and has been known to Indian cooking since at least 2000 BC. J. Innes

Miller notes that while pepper was grown in southern Thailand and in Malaysia, its most important source was India, particularly the Malabar Coast, in what is now the state of Kerala. Peppercorns were a much prized trade good, often referred to as 'black gold' and used as a form of commodity money. The term 'peppercorn rent' still exists today.

The ancient history of black pepper is often interlinked with (and confused with) that of long pepper, the dried fruit of closely related *Piper longum*. The Romans knew of both and often referred to either as just 'piper'. In fact, it was not until the discovery of the New World and of chile peppers that the popularity of long pepper entirely declined. Chile peppers, some of which when dried are similar in shape and taste to long pepper, were easier to grow in a variety of locations more convenient to Europe.

Until well after the Middle Ages, virtually all of the black pepper found in Europe, the Middle East, and North Africa travelled there from India's Malabar region. By the 16th century, pepper was also being grown in Java, Sunda, Sumatra, Madagascar, Malaysia, and elsewhere in Southeast Asia, but these areas traded mainly with China, or used the pepper locally. Ports in the Malabar area also served as a stop-off point for much of the trade in other spices from farther east in the Indian Ocean.

Black pepper, along with other spices from India and lands farther east, changed the course of world history. It was in some part the preciousness of these spices that led to the European efforts to find a sea route to India and consequently to the European colonial occupation of that country, as well as the European discovery and colonization of the Americas.

Black peppercorns were found stuffed in the nostrils of Ramesses II, placed there as part of the mummification rituals shortly after his death in 1213 BC. Little else is known about the use of pepper in ancient Egypt, nor how it reached the Nile from India.

Pepper (both long and black) was known in Greece at least as early as the 4th century BC, though it was probably an uncommon and expensive item that only the very rich could afford. Trade routes of the time were by land, or in ships which hugged the coastlines of the Arabian Sea. Long pepper, growing in the north-western part of India, was more accessible than the black pepper from further south; this trade advantage, plus long pepper's greater spiciness, probably made black pepper less popular at the time.

By the time of the early Roman Empire, especially after Rome's conquest of Egypt in 30 BC, open-ocean crossing of the Arabian Sea directly to southern India's Malabar Coast was near routine. Details of this trading across the Indian Ocean have been passed down in the *Periplus of the Erythraean Sea*. According to the Roman geographer Strabo, the early Empire sent a fleet of around 120 ships on an annual one-year trip to India and back. The fleet timed its travel across the Arabian Sea to take advantage of the predictable monsoon winds. Returning from India, the ships travelled up the Red Sea, from where the cargo was carried overland or via the Nile Canal to the Nile River, barged to Alexandria, and shipped from there to Italy and Rome. The rough geographical outlines of this same trade route would dominate the pepper trade into Europe for a millennium and a half to come.

With ships sailing directly to the Malabar coast, black pepper was now travelling a shorter trade route than long pepper, and the prices reflected it. Pliny the Elder's *Natural History* tells us the prices in Rome around 77 CE: "Long pepper ... is fifteen denarii per pound, while that of white pepper is seven, and of black, four." Pliny also complains "there is no year in which India does not drain the Roman Empire of fifty million sesterces," and further moralises on pepper.

It is quite surprising that the use of pepper has come so much into fashion, seeing that in other substances which we use, it is sometimes their sweetness, and sometimes their appearance that has attracted our notice; whereas, pepper has nothing in it that can plead as a recommendation to either fruit or berry, its only desirable quality being a certain pungency; and yet it is for this that we import it all the way from India! Who was the first to make trial of it as an article of food? and who, I wonder, was the man that was not content to prepare himself by hunger only for the satisfying of a greedy appetite? (*N.H.* 12.14)

Black pepper was a well-known and widespread, if expensive, seasoning in the Roman Empire. Apicius' De re coquinaria, a 3rd-century cookbook probably based at least partly on one from the 1st century CE, includes pepper in a majority of its recipes. Edward Gibbon wrote, in *The History of the Decline and Fall of the Roman Empire*, that pepper was "a favourite ingredient of the most expensive Roman cookery".

Postclassical Europe

Pepper was so valuable that it was often used as collateral or even currency. The taste for pepper (or the appreciation of its monetary value) was passed on to those who would see Rome fall. It is said that Alaric the Visigoth and Attila the Hun each demanded from Rome a ransom of more than a ton of pepper when they besieged the city in 5th century. After the fall of Rome, others took over the middle legs of the spice trade, first the Persians and then the Arabs; Innes Miller cites the account of Cosmas Indicopleustes, who travelled east to India, as proof that "pepper was still being exported from India in the sixth century". By the end of the Dark Ages, the central portions of the spice trade were firmly under Islamic control. Once into the Mediterranean, the trade was largely monopolised by Italian powers, especially Venice and Genoa. The rise of these city-states was funded in large part by the spice trade.

I am black on the outside, clad in a wrinkled cover, Yet within I bear a burning marrow. I season delicacies, the banquets of kings, and the luxuries of the table, Both the sauces and the tenderized meats of the kitchen. But you will find in me no quality of any worth, Unless your bowels have been rattled by my gleaming marrow.

It is commonly believed that during the Middle Ages, pepper was used to conceal the taste of partially rotten meat. There is no evidence to support this claim, and historians view it as highly unlikely: in the Middle Ages, pepper was a luxury item, affordable only to the wealthy, who certainly had unspoiled meat available as well. In addition, people of the time certainly knew that eating spoiled food would make them sick. Similarly, the belief that pepper was widely used as a preservative is questionable: it is true that piperine, the compound that gives pepper its spiciness, has some antimicrobial properties, but at the concentrations present when pepper is used as a spice, the effect is small. Salt is a much more effective preservative, and salt-cured meats were common fare, especially in winter. However, pepper and other spices probably did play a role in improving the taste of long-preserved meats.

Its exorbitant price during the Middle Ages — and the monopoly on the trade held by Italy — was one of the inducements which led the Portuguese to seek a sea route to India. In 1498, Vasco da Gama became the first European to reach India by sea; asked by Arabs in Calicut (who spoke Spanish and Italian) why they had come, his representative replied, “we seek Christians and spices.” Though this first trip to India by way of the southern tip of Africa was only a modest success, the Portuguese quickly returned in greater numbers and used their superior naval firepower to eventually gain complete control of trade on the Arabian sea. It was given additional legitimacy (at least from a European perspective) by the 1494 Treaty of Tordesillas, which granted Portugal exclusive rights to the half of the world where black pepper originated.

The Portuguese proved unable to maintain their stranglehold on the spice trade for long. The old Arab and Venetian trade networks successfully smuggled enormous quantities of spices through the patchy Portuguese blockade, and pepper once again flowed through Alexandria and Italy, as well as around Africa. In the 17th century, the Portuguese lost almost all of their valuable Indian Ocean possessions to the Dutch and the English. The pepper ports of Malabar fell to the Dutch in the period 1661-1663.

As pepper supplies into Europe increased, the price of pepper declined (though the total value of the import trade generally did not). Pepper, which in the early Middle Ages had been an item exclusively for the rich, started to become more of an everyday seasoning among those of more average means. Today, pepper accounts for one-fifth of the world's spice trade.

It is possible that black pepper was known in China in the 2nd century BC, if poetic reports regarding an explorer named Tang Meng (??) are correct. Sent by Emperor Wu to what is now south-west China, Tang Meng is said to have come across something called *jujiang* or 'sauce-betel'. He was told it came from the markets of Shu, an area in what is now the Sichuan province. The traditional view among historians is that 'sauce-betel' is a sauce made from betel leaves, but arguments have been made that it actually refers to pepper, either long or black.

In the 3rd century CE, black pepper made its first definite appearance in Chinese texts, as *hujiao* or 'foreign pepper'. It does not appear to have been widely known at the time, failing to appear in a 4th-century work describing a wide variety of spices from beyond China's southern border, including long pepper. By the 12th century, however, black pepper had become a popular ingredient in the cuisine of the wealthy and powerful, sometimes taking the place of China's native Sichuan pepper (the tongue-numbing dried fruit of an unrelated plant).

Marco Polo testifies to pepper's popularity in 13th-century China when he relates what he is told of its consumption in the city of Kinsay (Zhejiang): "... Messer Marco heard it stated by one of the Great Kaan's officers of customs that the quantity of pepper introduced daily for consumption into the city of Kinsay amounted to 43 loads, each load being equal to 223 lbs." Marco Polo is not considered a very reliable source regarding China, and this second-hand data may be even more suspect, but if this estimated 10,000 pounds (4,500 kg) a day for one city is anywhere near the truth, China's pepper imports may have dwarfed Europe's.

Like many eastern spices, pepper was historically both a seasoning and a medicine. Long pepper, being stronger, was often the preferred medication, but both were used.

Black peppercorns figure in remedies in Ayurveda, Siddha and Unani medicine in India. The 5th century *Syriac Book of Medicines* prescribes pepper (or perhaps long pepper) for such illnesses as constipation, diarrhoea, earache, gangrene, heart disease, hernia, hoarseness, indigestion, insect bites, insomnia, joint pain, liver problems, lung disease, oral abscesses, sunburn, tooth decay, and toothaches. Various sources from the 5th century onward also recommend pepper to treat eye problems, often by applying salves or poultices made with pepper directly to the eye. There is no current medical evidence that any of these treatments has any benefit; pepper applied directly to the eye would be quite uncomfortable and possibly damaging.

Pepper has long been believed to cause sneezing; this is still believed true today. Some sources say that piperine, a substance present in black pepper, irritates the nostrils, causing the sneezing; some say that it is just the effect of the fine dust in ground pepper, and some say that pepper is not in fact a very effective sneeze-producer at all. Few, if any, controlled studies have been carried out to answer the question. It has been shown that piperine can dramatically increase absorption of selenium, vitamin B and beta-carotene as well as other nutrients.

As a medicine, Pepper appears in the Buddhist Samaññaphala Sutta, chapter five, as one of the few medicines allowed to be carried by a monk.

Pepper contains small amounts of safrole, a mildly carcinogenic compound. Also, it is eliminated from the diet of patients having abdominal surgery and ulcers because of its irritating effect upon the intestines, being replaced by what is referred to as a bland diet.

Pepper gets its spicy heat mostly from the piperine compound, which is found both in the outer fruit and in the seed. Refined piperine, milligram-for-milligram, is about one per cent as hot as the capsaicin in chilli peppers. The outer fruit layer, left on black pepper, also contains important odour-contributing terpenes including pinene, sabinene, limonene, caryophyllene, and linalool, which give citrusy, woody, and floral notes. These scents are mostly missing in white pepper, which is stripped of the fruit layer. White pepper can gain some different odours (including musty notes) from its longer fermentation stage.

Pepper loses flavour and aroma through evaporation, so airtight storage helps preserve pepper's original spiciness longer. Pepper can also lose flavour when exposed to light, which can transform piperine into nearly tasteless isochavicine. Once ground, pepper's aromatics can evaporate quickly; most culinary sources recommend grinding whole peppercorns immediately before use for this reason. Handheld pepper mills (or 'pepper grinders'), which mechanically grind or crush whole peppercorns, are used for this, sometimes instead of pepper shakers, dispensers of pre-ground pepper. Spice mills such as pepper mills were found in European kitchens as early as the 14th century, but the mortar and pestle used earlier for crushing pepper remained a popular method for centuries after as well.

World Trade

Peppercorns are, by monetary value, the most widely traded spice in the world, accounting for 20 per cent of all spice imports in 2002. The price of pepper can be volatile, and this figure fluctuates a great deal year to year; for example, pepper made up 39 per cent of all spice imports in 1998. By weight, slightly more chilli peppers are traded worldwide than peppercorns. The International Pepper Exchange is located in Kochi, India.

As of 2008, Vietnam is the world's largest producer and exporter of pepper, producing 34 per cent of the worlds *Piper nigrum* crop as of 2008. Other major producers include Indonesia (9%), India (19%), Brazil (13%), Malaysia (8%), Sri Lanka (6%), Thailand (4%), and China (6%). Global pepper production peaked in 2003 with over 3,550,000 t (3,910,000 short tons), but has fallen to just over 2,710,000 t (2,990,000 short tons) by 2008 due to a series of issues including poor crop management, disease and weather. Vietnam dominates the export market, using almost none of its production domestically; however its 2007 crop fell by nearly 10 per cent from the previous year to about 90,000 t (99,000 short tons). Similar crop yields occurred in 2007 across the other pepper producing nations as well.

16 Tobacco

Tobacco is an agricultural product processed from the fresh leaves of plants in the genus *Nicotiana*. It can be consumed, used as an organic pesticide, and in the form of nicotine tartrate it is used in some medicines. In consumption it may be in the form of smoking, chewing, snuffing, dipping tobacco, or snus. Tobacco has long been in use as an entheogen in the Americas. However, upon the arrival of Europeans in North America, it quickly became popularized as a trade item and as a recreational drug. This popularization led to the development of the southern economy of the United States until it gave way to cotton. Following the American Civil War, a change in demand and a change in labour force allowed for the development of the cigarette. This new product quickly led to the growth of tobacco companies until the scientific controversy of the mid-1900s.

There are many species of tobacco, which are all encompassed by the plant genus *Nicotiana*. The word *nicotiana* (as well as *nicotine*) was named in honour of Jean Nicot, French ambassador to Portugal, who in 1559 sent it as a medicine to the court of Catherine de Medici.

Because of the addictive properties of nicotine, tolerance and dependence develop. Absorption quantity, frequency, and speed of tobacco consumption are believed to be directly related to biological strength of nicotine dependence, addiction, and tolerance. The usage of tobacco, is an activity that is practiced by some 1.1 billion people, and up to 1/3 of the adult population. The World Health Organization reports it to be the leading preventable cause of death worldwide and estimates that it currently causes 5.4 million deaths per year. Rates of smoking have levelled off or declined in developed countries, however they continue to rise in developing countries.

Tobacco is cultivated similar to other agricultural products. Seeds are sown in cold frames or hotbeds to prevent attacks from insects, and then transplanted into the fields. Tobacco is an annual crop, which is usually harvested in a large single-piece farm equipment. After harvest, tobacco is stored to allow for curing, which allow for the slow oxidation and degradation of carotenoids. This allows for the agricultural product to take on properties that are usually attributed to the 'smoothness' of the smoke. Following this, tobacco is packed into its various forms of consumption which include smoking, chewing, sniffing, and so on.

The Spanish word '*tabaco*' is thought to have its origin in Arawakan language, particularly, in the Taino language of the Caribbean. In Taino, it was said to refer either to a roll of tobacco leaves (according to Bartolome de Las Casas, 1552), or to the *tabago*, a kind of Y-shaped pipe for sniffing tobacco smoke (according to Oviedo; with the leaves themselves being referred to as *Cohiba*).

However, similar words in Spanish and Italian were commonly used from 1410 to define medicinal herbs, originating from the Arabic *tabbaq*, a word reportedly dating to the 9th century, as the name of various herbs.

Early Developments

Tobacco had already long been used in the Americas when European settlers arrived and introduced the practice to Europe, where it became popular. At high doses, tobacco can become hallucinogenic ; accordingly, Native Americans never used the drug recreationally. Instead, it was often consumed as an entheogen; among some tribes, this was done only by experienced shamans or medicine men. Eastern North American tribes would carry large amounts of tobacco in pouches as a readily accepted trade item and would often smoke it in pipes, either in defined ceremonies that were considered sacred, or to seal a bargain, and they would smoke it at such occasions in all stages of life, even in childhood. It was believed that tobacco was a gift from the Creator and that the exhaled tobacco smoke was capable of carrying one's thoughts and prayers to heaven.

Popularization

Following the arrival of the Europeans, tobacco became increasingly popular as a trade item. It fostered the economy for the southern United States until it was replaced by cotton. Following the American civil war, a change in demand and a change in labor force allowed inventor James Bonsack to create a machine which automated cigarette production.

This increase in production allowed tremendous growth in the tobacco industry until the scientific revelations of the mid-1900s.

Contemporary

Following the scientific revelations of the mid-1900s, tobacco became condemned as a health hazard, and eventually became encompassed as a cause for cancer, as well as other respiratory and circulatory diseases. This led to the Tobacco Master Settlement Agreement (MSA) which settled the lawsuit in exchange for a combination of yearly payments to the states and voluntary restrictions on advertising and marketing of tobacco products.

As the industry's downward tumble continued, in the 1990s Brown and Williamsons cross-bred a strain of tobacco to produce Y1. This strain of tobacco contained an unusually high amount of nicotine, nearly doubling its content from 3.2-3.5 per cent to 6.5 per cent. This prompted Food and Drug Administration (FDA) to use this strain as evidence that tobacco companies were intentionally manipulating the nicotine content of cigarettes.

In 2003, in response to tobaccos growth in developing countries, the World Health Organization (WHO) successfully rallied 168 countries to sign the Framework Convention on Tobacco Control. The Convention is designed to push for effective legislation and its enforcement in all countries to reduce the harmful effects of tobacco. This led to the development of tobacco cessation products.

Nicotiana

There are many species of tobacco, which are encompassed by the genus of herbs *Nicotiana*. It is part of the nightshade family (Solanaceae) indigenous to North and South America, Australia, south west Africa and the South Pacific.

Many plants contain nicotine, a powerful neurotoxin that is particularly harmful to insects. However, tobaccos contain a higher concentration of nicotine than most other plants. Unlike many other Solanaceae they do not contain tropane alkaloids, which are often poisonous to humans and other animals.

Despite containing enough nicotine and other compounds such as germacrene and anabasine and other piperidine alkaloids (varying between species) to deter most herbivores, a number of such animals have evolved the ability to feed on *Nicotiana* species without being harmed. Nonetheless, tobacco is unpalatable to many species and therefore some tobacco plants (chiefly Tree Tobacco, *N. glauca*) have become established as invasive weeds in some places are a number of types of tobacco include but are not limited to:

- **Aromatic Fire-cured**, it is cured by smoke from open fires. In the United States, it is grown in northern middle Tennessee, central Kentucky and in Virginia. Fire-cured tobacco grown in Kentucky and Tennessee are used in some chewing tobaccos, moist snuff, some cigarettes, and as a condiment in pipe tobacco blends. Another fire-cured tobacco is Latakia and is produced from oriental varieties of *N. tabacum*. The leaves are cured and smoked over smoldering fires of local hardwoods and aromatic shrubs in Cyprus and Syria.
- **Brightleaf tobacco**, Brightleaf is commonly known as 'Virginia tobacco', often regardless of which state they are planted. Prior to the American Civil War, most tobacco grown in the US was fire-cured dark-leaf. This type of tobacco was planted in fertile lowlands, used a robust variety of leaf, and was either fire cured or air cured. Most Canadian cigarettes are made from 100 per cent pure Virginia tobacco.
- **Burley tobacco**, is an air-cured tobacco used primarily for cigarette production. In the U.S., burley tobacco plants are started from palletized seeds placed in polystyrene trays floated on a bed of fertilized water in March or April.
- **Cavendish** is more a process of curing and a method of cutting tobacco than a type of it. The processing and the cut are used to bring out the natural sweet taste in the tobacco. Cavendish can be produced out of any tobacco type but is usually one of, or a blend of Kentucky, Virginia, and Burley and is most commonly used for pipe tobacco and cigars.
- **Criollo tobacco** is a type of tobacco, primarily used in the making of cigars. It was, by most accounts, one of the original Cuban tobaccos that emerged around the time of Columbus.
- **Dokham**, is a tobacco of Iranian origin mixed with leaves, bark, and herbs for smoking in a midwakh.

- **Oriental tobacco**, is a sun-cured, highly aromatic, small-leafed variety (*Nicotiana tabacum*) that is grown in Turkey, Greece, Bulgaria, and Macedonia. Oriental tobacco is frequently referred to as "Turkish tobacco", as these regions were all historically part of the Ottoman Empire. Many of the early brands of cigarettes were made mostly or entirely of Oriental tobacco; today, its main use is in blends of pipe and especially cigarette tobacco (a typical American cigarette is a blend of bright Virginia, burley and Oriental).
- **Perique**, A farmer called Pierre Chenet is credited with first turning this local tobacco into the Perique in 1824 through the technique of pressure-fermentation. Considered the truffle of pipe tobaccos, it is used as a component in many blended pipe tobaccos, but is too strong to be smoked pure. At one time, the freshly moist Perique was also chewed, but none is now sold for this purpose. It is typically blended with pure Virginia to lend spice, strength, and coolness to the blend.
- **Shade tobacco**, is cultivated in Connecticut and Massachusetts. Early Connecticut colonists acquired from the Native Americans the habit of smoking tobacco in pipes and began cultivating the plant commercially, even though the Puritans referred to it as the 'evil weed'. The industry has weathered some major catastrophes, including a devastating hailstorm in 1929, and an epidemic of brown spot fungus in 2000, but is now in danger of disappearing altogether, given the value of the land to real estate speculators.
- **White burley**, in 1865, George Webb of Brown County, Ohio planted Red Burley seeds he had purchased, and found that a few of the seedlings had a whitish, sickly look. The air-cured leaf was found to be more mild than other types of tobacco.

- **Wild tobacco**, is native to the southwestern United States, Mexico, and parts of South America. Its botanical name is *Nicotiana rustica*.
- **Y1** is a strain of tobacco that was cross-bred by Brown and Williamson to obtain an unusually high nicotine content. It became controversial in the 1990s when the United States Food and Drug Administration (FDA) used it as evidence that tobacco companies were intentionally manipulating the nicotine content of cigarettes.

Due to its long existence, tobacco has fostered many cultural items including: the usage of peace pipes, advertisements, movies. From its discovery tobacco has been highly regarded used in cultural ceremonies, for recreational purposes, and so forth. At the arrivals of the Europeans, tobacco was came to be regarded with wealth and knowledge. Smoking in public has for a long time been something reserved for men and when done by women has been associated with promiscuity. In Japan during the Edo period, prostitutes and their clients would often approach one another under the guise of offering a smoke and the same was true for 19th century Europe.

Following the civil war, the usage of tobacco, primarily in cigarettes became associated with masculinity, and power and is an iconic image associated with the stereotypical capitalist.From the mid-1900s and to today Tobacco is often rejected. This has spawned quitting-associations, negative-campaigns, and so forth. Bhutan is the only country in the world where tobacco sales are illegal.

Demographic

Research is limited mainly to tobacco smoking, which has been studied the more extensively than any other form of consumption. As of 2000, smoking is practiced by some 1.22 billion people, of which men are more likely to smoke than women (however the gender gap declines with age), poor more likely than rich, and people in developing countries or transitional economies are more likely than people in developed countries. As of 2004, the World Health Organization (WHO) reports that of the 58.8 million deaths to occur globally, 5.4 million are tobacco-attributed.

Tobacco use leads most commonly to diseases affecting the heart and lungs, with smoking being a major risk factor for heart attacks, chronic obstructive pulmonary disease (COPD), and cancer, particularly lung cancer, cancers of the larynx and mouth, and pancreatic cancer.

Fresh tobacco, processed tobacco, and tobacco smoke contain carcinogens. The current view on cancer is that carcinogenicity is a stochastic effect, where various environmental factors trigger the development of cancer. While exposure to a carcinogen increases the probability of cancer, the process remains random. For example, smoking tobacco is known to cause cancer in humans, but not all people who smoke necessarily develop smoking-related cancer. Additionally, in studies on humans, the large number of confounding variables makes it challenging to statistically distinguish their effects.

"Much of the disease burden and premature mortality attributable to tobacco use disproportionately affect the poor", and of the 1.22 billion smokers, 1 billion of them live in developing or transitional economies.

In Indonesia, the lowest income group spends 15 per cent of its total expenditures on tobacco. In Egypt, more than 10 per cent of households expediture in low-income homes is on tobacco. The poorest 20 per cent of households in Mexico spend 11 per cent of their income on tobacco.

The tobacco lobby gives money to politicians to vote in favor of deregulating tobacco. It is estimated that the United States tobacco lobby spends an average of $106,415 each day legislature meets; however the industry lost its support when the U.S. National Association of Attorneys General

(NAAG) filed charges against the Tobacco Institute, a tobacco industry advocacy group.

Cultivation

Tobacco is cultivated similar to other agricultural products. Seeds were at first quickly scattered onto the soil. However, young plants came under increasing attack from flea beetles (*Epitrix cucumeris* or *Epitrix pubescens*), which caused destruction of half the tobacco crops in United States in 1876. By 1890 successful experiments were conducted that placed the plant in a frame covered by thin fabric. Today, tobacco is sown in cold frames or hotbeds, as their germination is activated by light.

In the United States, tobacco is often fertilized with the mineral apatite, which partially starves the plant of nitrogen to produce a more desired flavor. Apatite, however, contains radium, lead 210, and polonium 210 — which are known radioactive carcinogens.

After the plants have reached relative maturity, they are transplanted into the fields, in which a relatively large hole is created in the tilled earth with a tobacco peg. Various mechanical tobacco planters where invented in the nineteenth and twentieth to automate the process: making the hole, fertilizing it, guiding the plant in — all in one motion.

Tobacco is cultivated annual, and can be harvested in several ways. In the oldest method, the entire plant is harvested at once by cutting off the stalk at the ground with a sickle. In the nineteenth century, bright tobacco began to be harvested by pulling individual leaves off the stalk as they ripened. The leaves ripen from the ground upwards, so a field of tobacco may go through several so-called 'pullings', more commonly known as topping (topping always refers to the removal of the tobacco flower before the leaves are systematically removed and, eventually, entirely harvested. As the industrial revolution took hold, harvesting wagons used to transport leaves were equipped with man-powered stringers, an apparatus which used twine to attach leaves to a pole. In modern times large fields are harvested by a single piece of farm equipment, although topping the flower and in some cases the plucking of immature leaves is still done by hand.

Curing and subsequent aging allows for the slow oxidation and degradation of carotenoids in tobacco leaf. This produces certain compounds in the tobacco leaves very similar and give a sweet hay, tea, rose oil, or fruity aromatic flavor that contribute to the "smoothness" of the smoke. Starch is converted to sugar which glycates protein and is oxidized into advanced glycation endproducts (AGEs), a caramelization process that also adds flavor. Inhalation of these AGEs in tobacco smoke contributes to atherosclerosis and cancer. Levels of AGE's is dependent on the curing method used.

Tobacco can be cured through several methods which include but are not limited to:

- **Air cured** tobacco is hung in well-ventilated barns and allowed to dry over a period of four to eight weeks. Air-cured tobacco is low in sugar, which gives the tobacco smoke a light, sweet flavor, and high in nicotine. Cigar and burley tobaccos are air cured.
- **Fire cured** tobacco is hung in large barns where fires of hardwoods are kept on continuous or intermittent low smoulder and takes between three days and ten weeks, depending on the process and the tobacco. Fire curing produces a tobacco low in sugar and high in nicotine. Pipe tobacco, chewing tobacco, and snuff are fire cured.
- **Flue cured** tobacco was originally strung onto tobacco sticks, which were hung from tier-poles in curing barns (Aus: kilns, also traditionally called Oasts). These barns have flues which run from externally fed fire boxes,

heat-curing the tobacco without exposing it to smoke, slowly raising the temperature over the course of the curing. The process will generally take about a week. This method produces cigarette tobacco that is high in sugar and has medium to high levels of nicotine.

- **Sun-cured** tobacco dries uncovered in the sun. This method is used in Turkey, Greece and other Mediterranean countries to produce oriental tobacco. Sun-cured tobacco is low in sugar and nicotine and is used in cigarettes.

Consumption

Beedi are thin, often flavored, south Asian cigarettes made of tobacco wrapped in a tendu leaf, and secured with colored thread at one end.

Chewing tobacco is one of the oldest ways of consuming tobacco leaves. It is consumed orally, in two forms: through sweetened strands, or in a shredded form. When consuming the long sweetened strands the tobacco is lightly chewed and compacted into a ball. When consuming the shredded tobacco, small amounts are placed at the bottom lip, between the gum and the teeth, where it is gently compacted, thus it can oftentimes be called *dipping tobacco.* Both methods stimulate the salve glands, which led to the development of the spittoon.

Cigars are tightly rolled bundle of dried and fermented tobacco which is ignited so that its smoke may be drawn into the smoker's mouth.

Cigarettes are a product consumed through the inhalation of smoke and manufactured out of cured and finely cut tobacco leaves and reconstituted tobacco, often combined with other additives, then rolled or stuffed into a paper-wrapped cylinder.

Creamy snuff are tobacco paste, consisting of tobacco, clove oil, glycerin, spearmint, menthol, and camphor, and sold in a toothpaste tube. It is marketed mainly to women in India, and is known by the brand names Ipco (made by Asha Industries), Denobac, Tona, Ganesh. It is locally known as 'mishri' in some parts of Maharashtra.

Dipping tobacco are a form of smokeless tobacco. Dip is occasionally referred to as 'chew', and because of this, it is commonly confused with chewing tobacco, which encompasses a wider range of products. A small clump of dip is 'pinched' out of the tin and placed between the lower or upper lip and gums.

Electronic cigarette is an alternative to tobacco smoking, although no tobacco is consumed. It is a battery-powered device that provides inhaled doses of nicotine by delivering a vapourized propylene glycol/nicotine solution.

Gutka are a preparation of crushed betel nut, tobacco, and sweet or savory flavorings. It is manufactured in India and exported to a few other countries. A mild stimulant, it is sold across India in small, individual-size packets.

Hookah are a single or multi-stemmed (often glass-based) water pipe for smoking. Originally from India, the hookah has gained immense popularity, especially in the middle east. A hookah operates by water filtration and indirect heat. It can be used for smoking herbal fruits, tobacco, or cannabis.

Kreteks are cigarettes made with a complex blend of tobacco, cloves and a flavoring 'sauce'. It was first introduced in the 1880s in Kudus, Java, to deliver the medicinal eugenol of cloves to the lungs.

Kreteks are cigarettes made with a complex blend of tobacco, cloves and a flavoring 'sauce'. It was first introduced in the 1880s in Kudus, Java, to deliver the medicinal eugenol of cloves to the lungs. Roll-Your-Own, often called rollies or roll ups, are very popular particularly in European countries. These are prepared from loose tobacco, cigarette papers and filters all bought separately. They are usually much cheaper to make. Pipe smoking typically consists of a small chamber (the bowl) for the combustion of the tobacco to be smoked and a thin stem (shank) that ends in a mouthpiece (the bit). Shredded pieces of tobacco are placed into the chamber and ignited. Snuff are a generic term for fine-ground smokeless tobacco products. Originally the term referred only to dry snuff, a fine tan dust popular mainly in the eighteenth century. Snuff powder originated in the UK town of Great Harwood and was famously ground in the town's monument prior to local distribution and transport further up north to Scotland. There are two major varieties which include European (dry) and American (moist); although American snuff is often referred to as dipping tobacco. Snus is steam-cured moist powder tobacco product that is not fermented and does not induce salivation. It is consumed by placing it in the mouth against the gums for an extended period of time. It is a form of snuff that is used in a manner similar to American dipping tobacco, but does not require regular spitting. Topical tobacco paste are sometimes recommended as a treatment for wasp, hornet, fire ant, scorpion, and bee stings. An amount equivalent to the contents of a cigarette is mashed in a cup with about a 0.5 to 1 teaspoon of water to make a paste that is then applied to the affected area. Tobacco water are traditional organic insecticide used in domestic gardening. Tobacco dust can be used similarly. It is produced by boiling strong tobacco in water, or by steeping the tobacco in water for a longer period. When cooled the mixture can be applied as a spray, or 'painted' on to the leaves of garden plants, where it will prove deadly to insects.

17 Sugarcane

Sugarcane (*Saccharum*) is a genus of 6 to 37 species (depending on taxonomic interpretation) of tall perennial grasses (family Poaceae, tribe Andropogoneae), native to warm temperate to tropical regions of the Old World. They have stout, jointed, fibrous stalks that are rich in sugar and measure 2 to 6 meters tall. All of the sugarcane species interbreed, and the major commercial cultivars are complex hybrids.

About 195 countries grow the crop to produce 1,324.6 million tons (more than six times the amount of sugar beet produced). As of the year 2005, the world's largest producer of sugarcane by far is Brazil followed by India. Uses of sugar cane include the production of sugar, Falernum, molasses, rum, soda, cachaça (the national spirit of Brazil) and ethanol for fuel. The bagasse that remains after sugarcane crushing may be burned to provide both heat - used in the mill — and electricity, typically sold to the consumer electricity grid. It may also, because of its high cellulose content, be used as raw material for paper, cardboard, and eating utensils branded as 'environmentally friendly' as it is made from a by-product of sugar production.

History of Sugarcane

The diffusion of sugarcane in pre-Islamic times (shown in red), in the mediaeval Muslim world (green) and by Europeans (violet).

Sugarcane was originally from tropical South Asia and Southeast Asia. Different species likely originated in different locations with *S. barberi* originating in India and *S. edule* and *S. officinarum* coming from New Guinea. The thick stalk stores energy as sucrose in the sap. From this juice, sugar is extracted by evaporating the water. Crystallized sugar was reported 5000 years ago in India.

Around the eighth century A.D., Arabs introduced sugar to the Mediterranean, Mesopotamia, Egypt, North Africa, and Spain. By the tenth century, sources state, there was no village in Mesopotamia that didn't grow sugarcane It was among the early crops brought to the Americas by Spaniards. Brazil is currently the biggest sugarcane producing country.

These houses were add-ons to the sugar plantations in the western colonies. This process was often conducted by the African slaves, under very poor conditions. The boiling house was made of cut stone. The furnaces were rectangular boxes of brick or stone with openings near to one side, and at the bottom to stoke the fire and pull out the ashes. At the top of each furnace were up to seven copper kettles or boilers, each one smaller than the previous one and hotter. The cane juice was placed in the first copper kettle which was the largest. The juice was then heated and a little lime added to remove impurities. The juice was then skimmed then channeled to the other copper kettles. The last kettle, which was called the 'teache' was where the cane juice became syrup. It was then put into cooling troughs where the sugar crystals hardened around a sticky core of molasses. The raw sugar was then shoveled from the cooling trough into hogsheads (wooden barrels) where they were put in the curing house.

Sugarcane was, and still is, extensively grown in the Caribbean, where it was first brought by Christopher Columbus during his second voyage to The Americas, initially to the island of Hispaniola (modern day Haiti and the Dominican Republic). In colonial times, sugar was a major product of the triangular trade of New World raw materials, European manufactures, and African slaves. France found its sugarcane islands so valuable it effectively traded its portion of Canada, famously dubbed 'a few acres of snow', to Britain for their return of Guadeloupe, Martinique and St. Lucia at the end of the Seven Years' War. The Dutch similarly kept Suriname, a sugar colony in South America, instead of seeking the return of the New Netherlands (New Amsterdam). Cuban sugarcane produced sugar that received price supports from and a guaranteed market in the USSR; the dissolution of that country forced the closure of most of Cuba's sugar industry. Sugarcane remains an important part of the economy of Belize, Barbados, Haiti along with the Dominican Republic, Guadeloupe, Jamaica, and other islands. The sugarcane industry is a major export for the Caribbean, but it is expected to collapse with the removal of European preferences by 2009.

Sugarcane production greatly influenced many tropical Pacific islands, including Okinawa and most particularly Hawaii and Fiji. In these islands, sugar cane came to dominate the economic and political landscape after the arrival of powerful European and American agricultural business, which promoted immigration from various Asian countries for workers to tend and harvest the crop. Sugar-industry policies eventually established the ethnic make-up of the island populations that now exist, profoundly affecting modern politics and society in the islands.

Brazil is a major grower of sugarcane, which is used to produce sugar and provide the ethanol used in making gasoline-ethanol blends (gasohol) for transportation fuel. In

India, sugarcane is sold as jaggery and also refined into sugar, primarily for consumption in tea and sweets, and for the production of alcoholic beverages.

Sugarcane cultivation requires a tropical or subtropical climate, with a minimum of 600 mm (24 in) of annual moisture. It is one of the most efficient photosynthesizers in the plant kingdom. It is a C-4 plant, able to convert up to 2 per cent of incident solar energy into biomass. In prime growing regions, such as Peru, Brazil, Bolivia, Colombia, Australia, Ecuador, Cuba, the Philippines and Hawaii, sugarcane can produce 20 kg for each square meter exposed to the sun.

Sugarcane is propagated from cuttings, rather than from seeds; although certain types still produce seeds, modern methods of stem cuttings have become the most common method of reproduction. Each cutting must contain at least one bud, and the cuttings are usually planted by hand. Once planted, a stand of cane can be harvested several times; after each harvest, the cane sends up new stalks, called *ratoons.* Usually, each successive harvest gives a smaller yield, and eventually the declining yields justify replanting. Depending on agricultural practice, two to ten harvests may be possible between plantings.

Sugarcane is harvested mostly by hand and sometimes mechanically. Hand harvesting accounts for more than half of the world's production, and is especially dominant in the developing world. When harvested by hand, the field is first set on fire. The fire spreads rapidly, burning away dry dead leaves, and killing any venomous snakes hiding in the crop, but leaving the water-rich stalks and roots unharmed. With cane knives or machetes, harvesters then cut the standing cane just above the ground. A skilled harvester can cut 500 kg of sugarcane in an hour.

With mechanical harvesting, a sugarcane combine (or chopper harvester), a harvesting machine originally developed in Australia, is used. The Austoft 7000 series was the original design for the modern harvester and has now been copied by other companies including Cameco and John Deere. The machine cuts the cane at the base of the stalk, separates the cane from its leaves, and deposits the cane into a haulout transporter while blowing the thrash back onto the field. Such machines can harvest 100 tonnes of cane each hour, but cane harvested using these machines must be transported to the processing plant rapidly; once cut, sugarcane begins to lose its sugar content, and damage inflicted on the cane during mechanical harvesting accelerates this decay.

Sugarcane is cultivated in almost all the world only for some months of the year.

Pests

The most important sugarcane pests are the larvae of some butterfly/moth species, including the turnip moth, the sugarcane borer (*Diatraea saccharalis*), the Mexican rice borer (*Eoreuma loftini*), leaf-cutting ants, termites; spittlebugs (especially *Mahanarva fimbriolata* and *Deois flavopicta*), and the beetle *Migdolus fryanus*. The planthopper *Eumetopina flavipes* is an insect which acts as a vector for the phytoplasma which causes the sugarcane disease ramu stunt.

Traditionally, sugarcane has been processed in two stages. Sugarcane mills, located in sugarcane-producing regions, extract sugar from freshly harvested sugarcane, resulting in raw sugar for later refining, and in "mill white" sugar for local consumption. Sugar refineries, often located in heavy sugar-consuming regions, such as North America, Europe, and Japan, then purify raw sugar to produce refined white sugar, a product that is more than 99 per cent pure sucrose. These two stages are slowly becoming blurred. Increasing affluence in the sugar-producing tropics has led to an increase in demand for refined sugar products in those areas, where a trend toward combined milling and refining has developed.

Milling

Sugarcane first has to be moved to a mill which is usually located close to the area of cultivation. Small rail networks are a common method of transporting the cane to a mill.Once the factories acquire the cane it will be subjected to the quality test. In Sri Lanka cane will be evaluated according to the brix and trash percentage.

In a sugar mill, sugarcane is washed, chopped, and shredded by revolving knives. The shredded cane is repeatedly mixed with water and crushed between rollers; the collected juices (called garapa in Brazil) contain 10-15 per cent sucrose, and the remaining fibrous solids, called bagasse, are burned for fuel. Bagasse makes a sugar mill more than self-sufficient in energy; the surplus bagasse can be used for animal feed, in paper manufacture, or burned to generate electricity for the local power grid.

The cane juice is next mixed with lime to adjust its pH to 7. This mixing arrests sucrose's decay into glucose and fructose, and precipitates out some impurities. The mixture then sits, allowing the lime and other suspended solids to settle out, and the clarified juice is concentrated in a multiple-effect evaporator to make a syrup about 60 per cent by weight in sucrose. This syrup is further concentrated under vacuum until it becomes supersaturated, and then seeded with crystalline sugar. Upon cooling, sugar crystallizes out of the syrup. A centrifuge is used to separate the sugar from the remaining liquid, or molasses. Additional crystallizations may be performed to extract more sugar from the molasses; the molasses remaining after no more sugar can be extracted from it in a cost-effective fashion is called blackstrap.

Raw sugar has a yellow to brown colour. If a white product is desired, sulfur dioxide may be bubbled through the cane juice before evaporation; this chemical bleaches many colour-forming impurities into colourless ones. Sugar bleached white by this *sulfitation* process is called 'mill white', 'plantation white', and 'crystal sugar'. This form of sugar is the form most commonly consumed in sugarcane-producing countries. Traditionally, sugarcane has been processed in two stages. Sugarcane mills, located in sugarcane-producing regions, extract sugar from freshly harvested sugarcane, resulting in raw sugar for later refining, and in 'mill white' sugar for local consumption. Sugar refineries, often located in heavy sugar-consuming regions, such as North America, Europe, and Japan, then purify raw sugar to produce refined white sugar, a product that is more than 99 per cent pure sucrose. These two stages are slowly becoming blurred. Increasing affluence in the sugar-producing tropics has led to an increase in demand for refined sugar products in those areas, where a trend toward combined milling and refining has developed.

Refining

Evaporator with baffled pan and foam dipper for making ribbon cane syrup. Three Rivers Historical Society Museum at Browntown, South Carolina.

In sugar refining, raw sugar is further purified. It is first mixed with heavy syrup and then centrifuged clean. This process is called 'affination'; its purpose is to wash away the outer coating of the raw sugar crystals, which is less pure than the crystal interior. The remaining sugar is then dissolved to make a syrup, about 70 per cent by weight solids.

The sugar solution is clarified by the addition of phosphoric acid and calcium hydroxide, which combine to precipitate calcium phosphate. The calcium phosphate particles entrap some impurities and absorb others, and then float to the top of the tank, where they can be skimmed off. An alternative to this 'phosphatation' technique is 'carbonatation,' which is similar, but uses carbon dioxide and calcium hydroxide to produce a calcium carbonate precipitate.

After any remaining solids are filtered out, the clarified syrup is decolourized by filtration through a bed of activated carbon; bone char was traditionally used in this role, but its use is no longer common. Some remaining colour-forming impurities adsorb to the carbon bed. The purified syrup is then concentrated to supersaturation and repeatedly crystallized under vacuum, to produce white refined sugar. As in a sugar mill, the sugar crystals are separated from the molasses by centrifuging. Additional sugar is recovered by blending the remaining syrup with the washings from affination and again crystallizing to produce brown sugar. When no more sugar can be economically recovered, the final molasses still contains 20-30 per cent sucrose and 15-25 per cent glucose and fructose.

To produce granulated sugar, in which the individual sugar grains do not clump together, sugar must be dried. Drying is accomplished first by drying the sugar in a hot rotary dryer, and then by conditioning the sugar by blowing cool air through it for several days.

Ribbon Cane Syrup

Ribbon cane is a subtropical type that was once widely grown in southern United States, as far north as coastal North Carolina. The juice was extracted with horse or mule-powered crushers; the juice was boiled, like maple syrup, in a flat pan, and then used in the syrup form as a sweetener for other foods. It is not a commercial crop nowadays, but a few growers try to keep alive the old traditions and find ready sales for their product. Most sugarcane production in the United States occurs in Florida and Louisiana, and to a lesser extent in Hawaii and Texas.

Cane Ethanol

This is generally available as a by-product of sugar mills producing sugar. It can be used as a fuel, mainly as a biofuel alternative to gasoline, and is widely used in cars in Brazil. It is steadily becoming a promising alternative to gasoline throughout much of the world and thus instead of sugar may be produced as a primary product out of sugar canes processing.

A textbook on renewable energy describes the energy transformation.

At present, 74 tons of raw sugar cane are produced annually per hectare in Brazil. The cane delivered to the processing plant is called burned and cropped (b & c) and represents 77 per cent of the mass of the raw cane. The reason for this reduction is that the stalks are separated from the leaves (which are burned and whose ashes are left in the field as fertilizer) and from the roots that remain in the ground to sprout for the next crop. Average cane production is, therefore, 58 tons of *b* and *c* per hectare per year.

Each ton of *b* and *c* yields 740 kg of juice (135 kg of sucrose and 605 kg of water) and 260 kg of moist bagasse (130 kg of dry bagasse). Since the higher heating value of sucrose is 16.5 MJ/kg, and that of the bagasse is 19.2 MJ/kg, the total heating value of a ton of *b* and *c* is 4.7 GJ of which 2.2 GJ come from the sucrose and 2.5 from the bagasse.

Per hectare per year, the biomass produced corresponds to 0.27 TJ. This is equivalent to 0.86 W per square meter. Assuming an average insolation of 225 W per square meter, the photosynthetic efficiency of sugar cane is 0.38 per cent.

The 135 kg of sucrose found in 1 ton of *b* and *c* are transformed into 70 liters of ethanol with a combustion energy of 1.7 GJ. The practical sucrose-ethanol conversion efficiency is, therefore, 76 per cent (compare with the theoretical 97%).

One hectare of sugar cane yields 4000 liters of ethanol per year (without any additional energy input because the bagasse produced exceeds the amount needed to distill the final product). This however does not include the energy used in tilling, transportation, and so on. Thus, the solar energy-to-ethanol conversion efficiency is 0.13 per cent.

Sugarcane as Food

In most countries where sugarcane is cultivated, there are several foods and popular dishes derived from it, such as:

Direct consumption of raw sugarcane cylinders or cubes, which are chewed to extract the juice, and the bagasse is spat out.

Freshly extracted juice (garapa, *guarab, guarapa, guarapo, papelón, 'aseer asab*, Ganna sharbat, mosto or *caldo de cana*) by hand or electrically operated small mills, with a touch of lemon and ice, makes a popular drink.

Molasses, used as a sweetener and as a syrup accompanying other foods, such as cheese or cookies.

Rapadura, a candy made of flavored solid brown sugar in Brazil, which can be consumed in small hard blocks, or in pulverized form (flour), as an add-on to other desserts.

Sugarcane is also used in rum production, especially in the Caribbean.

Cane sugar syrup was the traditional sweetener in soft drinks for many years, but has been largely supplanted (in the US at least) by high-fructose corn syrup, which is less expensive, but is considered by some to not taste quite like the sugar it replaces.

Hard rock candy is a confection that is enjoyed by people around the world.

Jaggery — solidified molasses of sugarcane, known as Gur or Gud in South Asia. Traditionally produced by heat evaporating sugarcane juice until it is a thick sludge and then letting it cool in buckets used as molds. Modern production methods make use of partial freeze drying to give reduce caramelization and give it lighter colour. It is used as sweetener in cooking traditional meal entrees as well as sweets and desserts.

Some sugarcane varieties are known to be capable of fixing atmospheric nitrogen in association with a bacterium, Acetobacter diazotrophicus. Unlike legumes and other nitrogen fixing plants which form root nodules in the soil in association with bacteria, Acetobacter diazotrophicus lives within the intercellular spaces of the sugarcane's stem.

Coffee

Coffee is a brewed beverage prepared from roasted seeds, commonly called coffee beans, of the coffee plant. Caffeinated coffee has a stimulating effect in humans. Today, coffee is one of the most popular beverages worldwide.

Coffee was first consumed in the ninth century, when it was discovered in the highlands of Ethiopia. From there, it spread to Egypt and Yemen, and by the 15th century, had reached Azerbaijan, Persia, Turkey, and northern Africa. From the Muslim world, coffee spread to Italy, then to the rest of Europe, to Indonesia, and to the Americas.

Coffee berries, which contain the coffee bean, are produced by several species of small evergreen bush of the genus *Coffea*. The two most commonly grown species are *Coffea canephora* (also known as *Coffea robusta*) and *Coffea arabica*. These are cultivated in Latin America, Southeast Asia, and Africa. Once ripe, coffee berries are picked, processed, and dried. The seeds are then roasted, undergoing several physical and chemical changes. They are roasted to varying degrees, depending on the desired flavour. They are then ground and brewed to create coffee. Coffee can be prepared and presented in a variety of ways.

Coffee has played an important role in many societies throughout modern history. In Africa and Yemen, it was used in religious ceremonies. As a result, the Ethiopian Church banned its secular consumption until the reign of Emperor Menelik II of Ethiopia. It was banned in Ottoman Turkey in the 17th century for political reasons, and was associated with rebellious political activities in Europe.

Coffee is an important export commodity. In 2004, coffee was the top agricultural export for 12 countries, and in 2005, it was the world's seventh-largest legal agricultural export by value.

Some controversy is associated with coffee cultivation and its impact on the environment. Many studies have examined the relationship between coffee consumption and certain medical conditions; whether the overall effects of coffee are positive or negative is still disputed.

The term was introduced to Europe via the Ottoman Turkish *kahve,* which is, in turn, derived from the Arabic: *qahweh.* The origin of the Arabic term is derived either from the name of the Kaffa region in western Ethiopia, where coffee was cultivated, or by a truncation of *qahwat al-bunn,* meaning 'wine of the bean' in Arabic. The English word *coffee* first came to be used in the early to mid-1600s, but early forms of the word date to the last decade of the 1500s. In Ethiopia's neighbour Eritrea, 'bunn' (also meaning 'wine of the bean' in Tigrinya) is used. Also the Amharic and Afan Oromo name for coffee is *bunna.*

History

Coffee use can be traced at least to as early as the ninth century, when it appeared in the highlands of Ethiopia. According to legend, Ethiopian shepherds were the first to observe the influence of the caffeine in coffee beans when the goats appeared to 'dance' and to have an increased level of energy after consuming wild coffee berries. The legend names the shepherd 'Kaldi'. From Ethiopia, coffee spread to Egypt and Yemen. It was in Arabia that coffee beans were first roasted and brewed, similar to how it is done today. By the 15th century, it had reached the rest of the Middle East, Persia, Turkey, and northern Africa.

In 1583, Leonhard Rauwolf, a German physician, gave this description of coffee after returning from a ten-year trip to the Near East:

> A beverage as black as ink, useful against numerous illnesses, particularly those of the stomach. Its consumers take it in the morning, quite frankly, in a porcelain cup that is passed around and from which each one drinks a cupful. It is composed of water and the fruit from a bush called bunnu.

From the Muslim world, coffee spread to Italy. The thriving trade between Venice and North Africa, Egypt, and the Middle East brought many goods, including coffee, to the Venetian port. From Venice, it was introduced to the rest of Europe. Coffee became more widely accepted after it was deemed a Christian beverage by Pope Clement VIII in 1600, despite appeals to ban the 'Muslim drink'. The first European coffee house opened in Italy in 1645. The Dutch were the first to import coffee on a large scale, and they were among the first to defy the Arab prohibition on the exportation of plants or unroasted seeds when Pieter van den Broeck smuggled seedlings from Aden into Europe in 1616. The Dutch later grew the crop in Java and Ceylon. The first exports of Indonesian coffee from Java to the Netherlands occurred in 1711. Through the efforts of the British East India Company, coffee became popular in England as well. It was introduced in France in 1657, and in Austria and Poland after the 1683 Battle of Vienna, when coffee was captured from supplies of the defeated Turks.

When coffee reached North America during the Colonial period, it was initially not as successful as it had been in Europe. During the Revolutionary War, however, the demand for coffee increased so much that dealers had to hoard their scarce supplies and raise prices dramatically; this was also due to the reduced availability of tea from British merchants. After the War of 1812, during which Britain temporarily cut off access to tea imports, the Americans' taste for coffee grew, and high demand during the American Civil War together with advances in brewing technology secured the position of coffee as an everyday commodity in the United States.

Noted as one of the world's largest, most valuable legally traded commodities (after oil), coffee has become a vital cash crop for many Third World countries. Over one hundred million people in developing countries have become dependent on coffee as their primary source of income (Ponte 1). Coffee has become the primary export and backbone for African countries like Uganda, Burundi, Rwanda, and Ethiopia as well as many Central American countries.

The *Coffea* plant is native to subtropical Africa and southern Asia. It belongs to a genus of ten species of flowering plants of the family *Rubiaceae*. It is an evergreen shrub or small tree that may grow 5 metres tall when unpruned. The leaves are dark green and glossy, usually 100–150, millimetres long and 60 millimetres wide. It produces clusters of fragrant white flowers that bloom simultaneously. The fruit berry is oval, about 15 millimetres long, and green when immature, but ripens to yellow, then crimson, becoming black on drying. Each berry usually contains two seeds, but from 5-10 per cent of the berries have only one; these are called peaberries. Berries ripen in seven to nine months.

Cultivation

Coffee is usually propagated by seeds. The traditional method of planting coffee is to put 20 seeds in each hole at the beginning of the rainy season; half are eliminated naturally. Coffee is often intercropped with food crops, such as corn, beans, or rice, during the first few years of cultivation.

The two main cultivated species of the coffee plant are *Coffea canephora* and *Coffea arabica*. Arabica coffee (from *C. arabica*) is considered more suitable for drinking than robusta coffee (from *C. canephora*); robusta tends to be bitter and have less flavour than arabica. For this reason, about three-quarters of coffee cultivated worldwide is *C. arabica*. However, *C. canephora* is less susceptible to disease than *C. arabica* and can be cultivated in environments where *C. arabica* will not thrive. Robusta coffee also contains about 40-50 per cent more caffeine than arabica. For this reason, it is used as an inexpensive substitute for arabica in many commercial coffee blends. Good quality robustas are used in some espresso blends to provide a better foam head and to lower the ingredient cost. Other cultivated species include *Coffea liberica* and *Coffea esliaca*, believed to be indigenous to Liberia and southern Sudan, respectively.

Most arabica coffee beans originate from either Latin America, eastern Africa, Arabia, or Asia. Robusta coffee beans are grown in western and central Africa, throughout southeast Asia, and to some extent in Brazil. Beans from different countries or regions usually have distinctive characteristics such as flavour, aroma, body, and acidity. These taste characteristics are dependent not only on the coffee's growing region, but also on genetic subspecies (varietals) and processing. Varietals are generally known by the region in which they are grown, such as Colombian, Java or Kona.

Originally, coffee farming was done in the shade of trees, which provided habitat for many animals and insects. This method is commonly referred to as the traditional shaded method. Many farmers have decided to switch their production method to sun cultivation, a method in which coffee is grown in rows under full sun with little or no forest canopy. This causes berries to ripen more rapidly and bushes to produce higher yields, but requires the clearing of trees and increased use of fertilizer and pesticides. Traditional coffee production, on the other hand, causes berries to ripen more slowly and produce lower yields, compared to the sun cultivation method, but the quality of the coffee is allegedly superior. In addition, the traditional shaded method is environment friendly and serves as a habitat for many species. Opponents of sun cultivation say environmental problems such as deforestation, pesticide pollution, habitat destruction, and soil and water degradation are the side effects of these practices. The American Birding Association has led a campaign for 'shade-grown' and organic coffees, which it says are sustainably harvested. However, while certain types of shaded coffee cultivation systems show greater biodiversity than full-sun systems, they still compare poorly to native forest in terms of habitat value.

Another issue concerning coffee is its use of water. According to New Scientist, it takes about 140 litres of water to grow the coffee beans needed to produce one cup of coffee, and the coffee is often grown in countries where there is a water shortage, such as Ethiopia.

Economics

Brazil remains the largest coffee exporting nation, but in recent years, Vietnam has become a major producer of robusta beans. Indonesia is the third-largest exporter and the largest producer of washed arabica coffee. Robusta coffees, traded in London at much lower prices than New York's arabica, are preferred by large industrial clients, such as multinational roasters and instant coffee producers because of the lower cost.

Coffee berries and their seeds undergo several processes before they become the familiar roasted coffee. First, coffee berries are picked, generally by hand. Then they are sorted by ripeness and colour and the flesh of the berry is removed, usually by machine, and the seeds—usually called beans—

are fermented to remove the slimy layer of mucilage still present on the bean. When the fermentation is finished, the beans are washed with large quantities of fresh water to remove the fermentation residue, which generates massive amounts of highly polluted coffee wastewater. Finally, the seeds are dried, sorted, and labelled as green coffee beans. A traditional way to let the coffee beans dry is to let them sit on a cement patio and rake over the beans till dry. Other companies use cylinders to pump in heated air to dry the coffee beans.

The next step in the process is the roasting of the green coffee. Coffee is usually sold in a roasted state, and all coffee is roasted before it is consumed. It can be sold roasted by the supplier, or it can be home roasted. The roasting process influences the taste of the beverage by changing the coffee bean both physically and chemically. The bean decreases in weight as moisture is lost and increases in volume, causing it to become less dense. The density of the bean also influences the strength of the coffee and requirements for packaging. The actual roasting begins when the temperature inside the bean reaches 200°C, though different varieties of beans differ in moisture and density and therefore roast at different rates. During roasting, caramelization occurs as intense heat breaks down starches in the bean, changing them to simple sugars that begin to brown, changing the colour of the bean. Sucrose is rapidly lost during the roasting process and may disappear entirely in darker roasts. During roasting, aromatic oils, acids, and caffeine weaken, changing the flavour; at 205°C, other oils start to develop. One of these oils is *caffeol*, created at about 200°C, which is largely responsible for coffee's aroma and flavour.

Depending on the colour of the roasted beans as perceived by the human eye, they will be labelled as light, medium light, medium, medium dark, dark, or very dark. A more accurate method of discerning the degree of roast involves measuring the reflected light from roasted beans illuminated with a light source in the near infrared spectrum. This elaborate light meter uses a process known as spectroscopy to return a number that consistently indicates the roasted coffee's relative degree of roast or flavour development. Such devices are routinely used for quality assurance by coffee-roasting businesses.

Darker roasts are generally smoother, because they have less fiber content and a more sugary flavour. Lighter roasts have more caffeine, resulting in a slight bitterness, and a stronger flavour from aromatic oils and acids otherwise destroyed by longer roasting times. A small amount of chaff is produced during roasting from the skin left on the bean after processing. Chaff is usually removed from the beans by air movement, though a small amount is added to dark roast coffees to soak up oils on the beans. Decaffeination may also be part of the processing that coffee seeds undergo. Seeds are decaffeinated when they are still green. Many methods can remove caffeine from coffee, but all involve either soaking beans in hot water or steaming them, then using a solvent to dissolve caffeine-containing oils. Decaffeination is often done by processing companies, and the extracted caffeine is usually sold to the pharmaceutical industry.

Storage

Once roasted, coffee beans must be stored properly to preserve the fresh taste of the bean. Ideally, the container must be airtight and kept cool. In order of importance, air, moisture, heat, and light are the environmental factors responsible for deteriorating flavour in coffee beans.

Folded-over bags, a common way consumers often purchase coffee, are generally not ideal for long-term storage because they allow air to enter. A better package contains a one-way valve, which prevents air from entering.

Preparation

Coffee beans must be ground and brewed in order to create a beverage. Grinding the roasted coffee beans is done at a roastery, in a grocery store, or in the home. They are most commonly ground at a roastery and then packaged and sold to the consumer, though 'whole bean' coffee can be ground at home. Coffee beans may be ground in several ways. A burr mill uses revolving elements to shear the bean, an electric grinder smashes the beans with blunt blades moving at high speed; and a mortar and pestle crushes the beans.

The type of grind is often named after the brewing method for which it is generally used. Turkish grind is the finest grind, while coffee percolator or French press are the coarsest grinds. The most common grinds are between the extremes; a medium grind is used in most common home coffee brewing machines.

Coffee may be brewed by several methods: boiled, steeped, or pressured. Brewing coffee by boiling was the earliest method, and Turkish coffee is an example of this method. It is prepared by powdering the beans with a mortar and pestle, then adding the powder to water and bringing it to a boil in a pot called a cezve or, in Greek, a briki. This produces a strong coffee with a layer of foam on the surface.

Machines such as percolators or automatic coffeemakers brew coffee by gravity. In an automatic coffeemaker, hot water drips onto coffee grounds held in a coffee filter made of paper or perforated metal, allowing the water to seep through the ground coffee while absorbing its oils and essences. Gravity causes the liquid to pass into a carafe or pot while the used coffee grounds are retained in the filter. In a percolator, boiling water is forced into a chamber above a filter by steam pressure created by boiling. The water then passes downward through the grounds due to gravity, repeating the process until shut off by an internal timer or, more commonly, a thermostat that turns off the heater when the entire pot reaches a certain temperature. This thermostat also serves to keep the coffee warm (it turns on when the pot cools), but requires the removal of the basket holding the grounds after the initial brewing to avoid additional brewing as the pot reheats. Purists do not feel that this repeated boiling is conducive to achieving the best-flavoured coffee.

Coffee may also be brewed by steeping in a device such as a French press (also known as a *cafetière* or coffee press). Ground coffee and hot water are combined in a coffee press and left to brew for a few minutes. A plunger is then depressed to separate the coffee grounds, which remain at the bottom of the container. Because the coffee grounds are in direct contact with the water, all the coffee oils remain in the beverage, making it stronger and leaving more sediment than in coffee made by an automatic coffee machine.

The espresso method forces hot (but not boiling) pressurized water through ground coffee. As a result of brewing under high pressure (ideally between 9-10 atm), the espresso beverage is more concentrated (as much as 10 to 15 times the amount of coffee to water as gravity-brewing methods can produce) and has a more complex physical and chemical constitution. A well-prepared espresso has a reddish-brown foam called *crema* that floats on the surface. The drink 'Americano' is popularly thought to have been named after American soldiers in WW II who found the European way of drinking espresso too strong, baristas would cut the espresso with hot water for them.

Once brewed, coffee may be presented in a variety of ways. Drip brewed, percolated, or French-pressed/cafetière coffee may be served with no additives or sugar (colloquially known as black) or with milk, cream, or both. When served cold, it is called iced coffee.

Espresso-based coffee has a wide variety of possible presentations. In its most basic form, it is served alone as a 'shot' or in the more watered-down style café américano—a shot or two of espresso with hot water. The Americano should be served with the espresso shots on top of the hot water to preserve the crema. Milk can be added in various forms to espresso: steamed milk makes a cafè latte, equal parts espresso and milk froth make a cappuccino and a dollop of hot foamed milk on top creates a caffè macchiato. The use of steamed milk to form patterns such as hearts or maple leaves is referred to as latte art.

A number of products are sold for the convenience of consumers who do not want to prepare their own coffee. Instant coffee is dried into soluble powder or freeze-dried into granules that can be quickly dissolved in hot water. Canned coffee has been popular in Asian countries for many years, particularly in Japan and South Korea. Vending machines typically sell varieties of flavoured canned coffee, much like brewed or percolated coffee, available both hot and cold. Japanese convenience stores and groceries also have a wide availability of bottled coffee drinks, which are typically lightly sweetened and preblended with milk. Bottled coffee drinks are also consumed in the United States. Liquid coffee concentrates are sometimes used in large institutional situations where coffee needs to be produced for thousands of people at the same time. It is described as having a flavour about as good as low-grade robusta coffee, and costs about 10¢ a cup to produce. The machines used can process up to 500 cups an hour, or 1,000 if the water is preheated.

Coffee was initially used for spiritual reasons. At least 1,000 years ago, traders brought coffee across the Red Sea into Arabia (modern-day Yemen), where Muslim monks began cultivating the shrub in their gardens. At first, the Arabians made wine from the pulp of the fermented coffee berries. This beverage was known as *qishr* (*kisher* in modern usage) and was used during religious ceremonies.

Coffee became the substitute beverage in spiritual practices where wine was forbidden. Coffee drinking was briefly prohibited by Muslims as *haraam* in the early years of the 16th century, but this was quickly overturned. Use in religious rites among the Sufi branch of Islam led to coffee's being put on trial in Mecca: it was accused of being a heretical substance, and its production and consumption were briefly repressed. It was later prohibited in Ottoman Turkey under an edict by the Sultan Murad IV. Coffee, regarded as a Muslim drink, was prohibited by Ethiopian Orthodox Christians until as late as 1889; it is now considered a national drink of Ethiopia for people of all faiths. Its early association in Europe with rebellious political activities led to its banning in England, among other places.

A contemporary example of coffee prohibition can be found in The Church of Jesus Christ of Latter-day Saints. The organization claims that it is both physically and spiritually unhealthy to consume coffee. This comes from the Mormon doctrine of health, given in 1833 by Mormon founder Joseph Smith in a revelation called the Word of Wisdom. It does not identify coffee by name, but includes the statement that 'hot drinks are not for the belly', which has been interpreted to forbid both coffee and tea to avoid tea and coffee and other stimulants. Studies conducted on Adventists have shown a small but statistically significant association between coffee consumption and mortality from ischemic heart disease, other cardiovascular disease, all cardiovascular diseases combined, and all causes of death.

Health and Pharmacology

Coffee ingestion on average is about a third of that of tap water in North America and Europe Worldwide, 6.7 million metric tons of coffee were produced annually in 1998-2000, and the forecast is a rise to 7 million metric tons annually by 2010.

Scientific studies have examined the relationship between coffee consumption and an array of medical conditions. Findings are contradictory as to whether coffee has any specific health benefits, and results are similarly conflicting regarding the negative effects of coffee consumption.

Coffee consumption has been linked to breast size reduction, and taking regular hits of caffeine reduces the risk of breast cancer. Coffee appears to reduce the risk of Alzheimer's disease, Parkinson's disease, heart disease, diabetes mellitus type 2, cirrhosis of the liver, and gout. A longitudinal study in 2009 showed that moderate drinkers of coffee (3-5 cups per day) had lower chances of getting Dementia, in addition to Alzheimer's disease . It increases the risk of acid reflux and associated diseases. Some health effects of coffee are due to its caffeine content, as the benefits are only observed in those who drink caffeinated coffee while others appear to be due to other components. For example, the antioxidants in coffee prevent free radicals from causing cell damage.

Coffee consumption can lead to iron deficiency anaemia in mothers and infants. Coffee also interferes with the absorption of supplemental iron.

American scientist Yaser Dorri has suggested that the smell of coffee can restore appetite and refresh olfactory receptors. He suggests that people can regain their appetite after cooking by smelling coffee beans, and that this method can also be used for research animals. Many high end perfume shops now offer coffee beans to refresh the receptors between perfume tests.

Over 1,000 chemicals have been reported in roasted coffee; more than half of those tested (19/28) are rodent carcinogens. Coffee's negative health effects are often blamed on its caffeine content. Research suggests that drinking caffeinated coffee can cause a temporary increase in the stiffening of arterial walls. Coffee is no longer thought to be a risk factor for coronary heart disease. Some studies suggest that it may have a mixed effect on short-term memory, by improving it when the information to be recalled is related to the current train of thought but making it more difficult to recall unrelated information. About 10 per cent of people with a moderate daily intake (235 mg per day) reported increased depression and anxiety when caffeine was withdrawn, and about 15 per cent of the general population report having stopped caffeine use completely, citing concern about health and unpleasant side effects.

Caffeine Content

Depending on the type of coffee and method of preparation, the caffeine content of a single serving can vary greatly. On average, a single cup of coffee (about 207 millilitres or a single shot of espresso (about 30 ml) can be expected to contain the following amounts of caffeine:

- ***Drip coffee:*** 115-175 mg (0.56-0.85 mg/ml)
- ***Espresso:*** 60 mg (2 mg/ml)
- ***Brewed/Pressed:*** 80-135 mg (0.39-0.65 mg/ml)
- ***Instant:*** 65-100 mg (0.31-0.48 mg/ml)
- ***Decaf, brewed:*** 3-4 mg
- ***Decaf, instant:*** 2-3 mg.

19 Cotton

Cotton is a soft, staple fiber that grows in a form known as a boll around the seeds of the cotton plant a shrub native to tropical and subtropical regions around the world, including the Americas, India and Africa. The fiber most often is spun into yarn or thread and used to make a soft, breathable textile, which is the most widely used natural-fiber cloth in clothing today. The English name, which began to be used circa 1400, derives from the Arabic *(al) qutn*, meaning cotton.

Cotton was cultivated by the inhabitants of the Indus Valley Civilization by the 5th millennium BCE — 4th millennium BCE. The Indus cotton industry was well developed and some methods used in cotton spinning and fabrication continued to be used until the modern Industrialization of India. Well before the Common Era the use of cotton textiles had spread from India to the Mediterranean and beyond.

According to The Columbia Encyclopedia, Sixth Edition:

> "Cotton has been spun, woven, and dyed since prehistoric times. It clothed the people of ancient India, Egypt, and China. Hundreds of years before the

Christian era cotton textiles were woven in India with matchless skill, and their use spread to the Mediterranean countries. In the 1st century. Arab traders brought fine muslin and calico to Italy and Spain. The Moors introduced the cultivation of cotton into Spain in the 9th century. Fustians and dimities were woven there and in the 14th century in Venice and Milan, at first with a linen warp. Little cotton cloth was imported to England before the 15th century, although small amounts were obtained chiefly for candlewicks. By the 17th century the East India Company was bringing rare fabrics from India. Native Americans skillfully spun and wove cotton into fine garments and dyed tapestries. Cotton fabrics found in Peruvian tombs are said to belong to a pre-Inca culture. In colour and texture the ancient Peruvian and Mexican textiles resemble those found in Egyptian tombs."

The earliest cultivation of cotton discovered thus far in the Americas occurred in Mexico, some 5,000 years ago. The indigenous species was *Gossypium hirsutum* which is today the most widely planted species of cotton in the world, constituting about 90 per cent of all production worldwide. The greatest diversity of wild cotton species is found in Mexico, followed by Australia and Africa.

In Iran (Persia), the history of cotton dates back to Achaemenid era (5th century B.C.), however there are few sources about the implantation of cotton in Pre-Islamic Iran. The implantation of cotton was common in Merv, Ray and Pars of Iran (Persia). In the poems of Persian poets, specially Ferdowsi's Shahname, there are many referrals to Cotton ('Panbe' in Persian). Marco Polo (13th century) refers to the major products of Persia (Iran), including Cotton. John Chardin a famous french traveler of 17th century who has visited the Safavid Persia, has approved the vast cotton farms of Persia.

In Peru, cultivation of the indigenous cotton species *Gossypium barbadense* was the backbone of the development of coastal cultures such as the Norte Chico, Moche and Nazca. Cotton was grown upriver, made into nets and traded with fishing villages along the coast for large supplies of fish. The Spanish who came to Mexico in the early 1500s found the people growing cotton and wearing clothing made of it.

During the late mediaeval period, cotton became known as an imported fiber in northern Europe, without any knowledge of how it was derived, other than that it was a plant; noting its similarities to wool, people in the region could only imagine that cotton must be produced by plant-borne sheep. John Mandeville, writing in 1350, stated as fact the now-preposterous belief: "There grew there [India] a wonderful tree which bore tiny lambs on the endes of its branches. These branches were so pliable that they bent down to allow the lambs to feed when they are hungrie [*sic*]." (See Vegetable Lamb of Tartary.) This aspect is retained in the name for cotton in many European languages, such as German *Baumwolle*, which translates as 'tree wool' (*Baum* means 'tree'; *Wolle* means 'wool'). By the end of the 16th century, cotton was cultivated throughout the warmer regions in Asia and the Americas.

India's cotton-processing sector gradually declined during British expansion in India and the establishment of colonial rule during the late 18th and early 19th centuries. This was largely due to the East India Company's exposing of India to foreign competition, which made cotton processing and manufacturing workshops in India uncompetitive. Indian markets increasingly supplied only raw cotton and were obliged to purchase manufactured textiles from Britain.

The advent of the Industrial Revolution in Britain provided a great boost to cotton manufacture, as textiles emerged as Britain's leading export. In 1738 Lewis Paul and John Wyatt, of Birmingham, England, patented the Roller Spinning machine, and the flyer-and-bobbin system for drawing cotton to a more even thickness using two sets of rollers that travelled at different speeds. Later, the invention of the spinning jenny in 1764 and Richard Arkwright's spinning frame (based on the Roller Spinning Machine) in 1769 enabled British weavers to produce cotton yarn and cloth at much higher rates. From the late eighteenth century onwards, the British city of Manchester acquired the nickname *'cottonopolis'* due to the cotton industry's omnipresence within the city, and Manchester's role as the heart of the global cotton trade. Production capacity was further improved by the invention of the cotton gin by Eli Whitney in 1793. Improving technology and increasing control of world markets allowed British traders to develop a commercial chain in which raw cotton fibers were (at first) purchased from colonial plantations, processed into cotton cloth in the mills of Lancashire, and then re-exported on British ships to captive colonial markets in West Africa, India, and China (via Shanghai and Hong Kong).

By the 1840s, India was no longer capable of supplying the vast quantities of cotton fibers needed by mechanized British factories, while shipping bulky, low-price cotton from India to Britain was time-consuming and expensive. This, coupled with the emergence of American cotton as a superior type (due to the longer, stronger fibers of the two domesticated native American species, *Gossypium hirsutum* and *Gossypium barbadense*), encouraged British traders to purchase cotton from plantations in the United States and the Caribbean. This was also much cheaper as it was produced by unpaid slaves. By the mid 19th century, 'King Cotton' had become the backbone of the southern American economy. In the United States, cultivating and harvesting cotton became the leading occupation of slaves.

During the American Civil War, American cotton exports slumped due to a Union blockade on Southern ports, also because of a strategic decision by the Confederate Government to cut exports, hoping to force Britain to recognize the Confederacy or enter the war, prompting the main purchasers of cotton, Britain and France, to turn to Egyptian cotton. British and French traders invested heavily in cotton plantations and the Egyptian government of Viceroy Isma'il took out substantial loans from European bankers and stock exchanges. After the American Civil War ended in 1865, British and French traders abandoned Egyptian cotton and returned to cheap American exports, sending Egypt into a deficit spiral that led to the country declaring bankruptcy in 1876, a key factor behind Egypt's annexation by the British Empire in 1882.

During this time cotton cultivation in the British Empire, especially India, greatly increased to replace the lost production of the American South. Through tariffs and other restrictions the British government discouraged the production of cotton cloth in India; rather the raw fiber was sent to England for processing. The Indian patriot Mahatma Gandhi described the process:

English people buy Indian cotton in the field, picked by Indian labour at seven cents a day, through an optional monopoly.

This cotton is shipped on British bottoms, a three-week journey across the Indian Ocean, down the Red Sea, across the Mediterranean, through Gibraltar, across the Bay of Biscay and the Atlantic Ocean to London. One hundred per cent profit on this freight is regarded as small.

The cotton is turned into cloth in Lancashire. You pay shilling wages instead of Indian pennies to your workers. The English worker not only has the advantage of better wages, but the steel companies of England get the profit of building the factories and machines. Wages, profits, all these are spent in England.

The finished product is sent back to India at European shipping rates, once again on British ships. The captains, officers, sailors of these ships, whose wages must be paid, are English. The only Indians who profit are a few lascars who do the dirty work on the boats for a few cents a day.

The cloth is finally sold back to the kings and landlords of India who got the money to buy this expensive cloth out of the poor peasants of India who worked at seven cents a day.

In the United States, Southern cotton provided capital for the continuing development of the North. The cotton produced by enslaved African Americans not only helped the South but also enriched Northern merchants. Much of the Southern cotton was transshipped through the northern ports.

Cotton remained a key crop in the southern economy after emancipation and the end of the civil war in 1865. Across the South, sharecropping evolved, in which free black farmers worked on white-owned cotton plantations in return for a share of the profits. Cotton plantations required vast labour forces to hand-pick cotton, and it was not until the 1950s that reliable harvesting machinery was introduced into the South (prior to this, cotton-harvesting machinery had been too clumsy to pick cotton without shredding the fibers). During the early twentieth century, employment in the cotton industry fell as machines began to replace labourers, and as the South's rural labour force dwindled during the First and Second World Wars. Today, cotton remains a major export of the southern United States, and a majority of the world's annual cotton crop is of the long-staple American variety.

In 1901, Peru's cotton industry suffered because of a fungus plague caused by a plant disease known as 'Cotton wilt' and 'Fusarium wilt' (Fusarium vasinfectum). The plant disease, which spread throughout Peru, entered the plant by its roots and worked its way up the stem until the plant was completely dried up. Fermín Tangüis a Puerto Rican agriculturist who lived in Peru, studied some species of the plant that were affected by the disease to a lesser extent and experimented in germination with the seeds of various cotton plants. In 1911, after 10 years of experimenting and failures, Tangüis was able to develop a seed which produced a superior cotton plant resistant to the disease. The seeds produced a plant that had a 40 per cent longer (between 29 mm and 33 mm) and thicker fiber that did not break easily and required little water. The Tangüis cotton, as it became known, is the variety which is preferred by the Peruvian national textile industry. It constituted 75 per cent of all the Peruvian cotton production, both for domestic use and apparel exports. The Tangüis cotton crop was estimated at 225,000 bales that year.

Cultivation

Successful cultivation of cotton requires a long frost-free period, plenty of sunshine, and a moderate rainfall, usually from 600 to 1200mm (24 to 48 inches). Soils usually need to be fairly heavy, although the level of nutrients does not need to be exceptional. In general, these conditions are met within the seasonally dry tropics and subtropics in the Northern and Southern hemispheres, but a large proportion of the cotton grown today is cultivated in areas with less rainfall that obtain the water from irrigation. Production of the crop for a given year usually starts soon after harvesting the preceding autumn. Planting time in spring in the Northern hemisphere varies from the beginning of February to the beginning of June. The area of the United States known as the South Plains is the largest contiguous cotton-growing region in the world. It is heavily dependent on irrigation water drawn from the Ogallala Aquifer.

Cotton is a thirsty crop, and as water resources get tighter around the world, economies that rely on it face difficulties and conflict, as well as potential environmental problems. For example, cotton has led to desertification in areas of Uzbekistan, where it is a major export. In the days of the Soviet Union, the Aral Sea was tapped for agricultural irrigation, largely of cotton, and now salination is widespread.

Genetically modified (GM) cotton was developed to reduce the heavy reliance on pesticides. The bacterium Bacillus thuringiensis naturally produces a chemical harmful only to a small fraction of insects, most notably the larvae of moths and butterflies, beetles, and flies, and harmless to other forms of life. The gene coding for BT toxin has been inserted into cotton, causing cotton to produce this natural insecticide in its tissues. In many regions the main pests in commercial cotton are lepidopteran larvae, which are killed by the BT protein in the transgenic cotton that they eat. This eliminates the need to use large amounts of broad-spectrum insecticides to kill lepidopteran pests (some of which have developed pyrethroid resistance). This spares natural insect predators in the farm ecology and further contributes to non-insecticide pest management.

BT cotton is ineffective against many cotton pests, however, such as plant bugs, stink bugs, aphids, etc.; depending on circumstances it may still be desirable to use insecticides against these.

Genetically modified cotton is widely used throughout the world. However, researchers have recently published the first documented case of in-field pest resistance to GM cotton. The International Service for the Acquisition of Agri-biotech Applications (ISAAA) said that, worldwide, GM cotton was planted on an area of 67,000 km^2 in 2002. This is 20 per cent of the worldwide total area planted in cotton. The U.S. cotton crop was 73 per cent GM in 2003.

The initial introduction of GM cotton proved to be a commercial and ecological disaster in Australia — the yields were far lower than predicted, and the cotton plants were cross-pollinated with other varieties of cotton. However, the introduction of a second variety of GM cotton led to 15 per cent of Australian cotton being GM in 2003. 80 per cent of the crop was genetically modified in 2004, when the original GM variety was banned.

Cotton has also been genetically modified for resistance to glyphosate (marketed as Roundup in the USA), an inexpensive and highly effective but broad-spectrum herbicide, during its early growth. This allows glyphosate to be used for weed control during the early growing season.

GM cotton acreage in India continues to grow at a rapid rate increasing from 50,000 hectares in 2002 to 3.8 million hectares in 2006. The total cotton area in India is about 9.0 million hectares (the largest in the world or, about 25 per cent of world cotton area) so GM cotton is now grown on 42 per cent of the cotton area. This makes India the country with the largest area of GM cotton in the world, surpassing China (3.5 million hectares in 2006). The major reasons for this increase is a combination of increased farm income ($225/ha) and a reduction in pesticide use to control the Cotton Bollworm.

Organic Cotton

Organic cotton is cotton that is grown without insecticide or pesticide. Worldwide, cotton is a pesticide-intensive crop, using approximately 25 per cent of the world's insecticides and 10 per cent of the world's pesticides. According to the World Health Organization (WHO), 20,000 deaths occur each year from pesticide poisoning in developing countries, many of these from cotton farming. Organic agriculture uses methods that are ecological, economical, and socially sustainable and denies the use of agrochemicals and artificial fertilizers. Instead, organic agriculture uses crop rotation, the growing of different crops than cotton in alternative years. The use of insecticides is prohibited; organic agriculture uses natural enemies to suppress harmful insects. The production of organic cotton is more expensive than the production of conventional cotton. Although toxic pollution from synthetic chemicals is eliminated, other pollution-like problems may remain, particularly run-off. Organic cotton is produced in organic agricultural systems that produce food and fiber according to clearly established standards. Organic agriculture prohibits the use of toxic and persistent chemical pesticides and fertilizers, as well as genetically modified organisms. It seeks to build biologically diverse agricultural systems, replenish and maintain soil fertility, and promote a healthy environment.

The cotton industry relies heavily on chemicals such as fertilizers and insecticides, although a very small number of farmers are moving toward an organic model of production and organic cotton products are now available for purchase at limited locations. These are popular for baby clothes and diapers. Under most definitions, organic products do not use genetic engineering.

Historically, in North America, one of the most economically destructive pests in cotton production has been the boll weevil. Due to the US Department of Agriculture's highly successful Boll Weevil Eradication Programme (BWEP), this pest has been eliminated from cotton in most of the United States. This programme, along with the introduction of genetically engineered 'Bt cotton' (which contains a bacteria gene that codes for a plant-produced protein that is toxic to a number of pests such as tobacco budworm, cotton bollworm, and pink bollworm), has allowed a reduction in the use of synthetic insecticides.

Cotton has gossypol, a toxin that makes it inedible. However, scientists have silenced the gene that produces the toxin, making it a potential food crop.

Most cotton in the United States, Europe, and Australia is harvested mechanically, either by a cotton picker, a machine that removes the cotton from the boll without damaging the cotton plant, or by a cotton stripper, which strips the entire boll off the plant. Cotton strippers are used in regions where it is too windy to grow picker varieties of cotton, and usually after application of a chemical defoliant or the natural defoliation that occurs after a freeze. Cotton is a perennial crop in the tropics and without defoliation or freezing, the plant will continue to grow.

Competition from Synthetic Fibers

The era of manufactured fibers began with the development of Rayon in France in the 1890s. Rayon is derived from a natural cellulose and cannot be considered synthetic, but requires extensive processing in a manufacturing process and led the less expensive replacement of more naturally derived materials. A succession of new synthetic fibers were introduced by the chemicals industry in the following decades. Acetate in fiber form was developed in 1924. Nylon, the first fiber synthesized entirely from petrochemicals, was introduced as a sewing thread by DuPont in 1936, followed by Dupont's acrylic in 1944. Some garments were created from fabrics based on these fibers, such as women's hosiery from nylon, but it was not until the introduction of polyester into the fiber marketplace in the early 1950s that the market for cotton came under threat. The rapid uptake of polyester garments in the 1960s caused economic hardship in cotton exporting economies, especially in Central American countries such as Nicaragua where cotton production had boomed ten-fold between 1950 and 1965 with the advent of cheap chemical pesticides. Cotton production recovered in the 1970s, but crashed to pre-1960 levels in the early 1990s.

The era of manufactured fibers began with the development of Rayon in France in the 1890s. Rayon is derived from a natural cellulose and cannot be considered synthetic, but requires extensive processing in a manufacturing process and led the less expensive replacement of more naturally derived materials. A succession of new synthetic fibers were introduced by the chemicals industry in the following decades. Acetate in fiber form was developed in 1924. Nylon, the first fiber synthesized entirely from petrochemicals, was introduced as a sewing thread by DuPont in 1936, followed by Dupont's acrylic in 1944. Some garments were created from fabrics based on these fibers, such as women's hosiery from nylon, but it was not until the introduction of polyester into the fiber marketplace in the early 1950s that the market for cotton came under threat. The rapid uptake of polyester garments in the 1960s caused economic hardship in cotton exporting economies, especially in Central American countries such as Nicaragua where cotton production had boomed tenfold between 1950 and 1965 with the advent of cheap chemical pesticides. Cotton production recovered in the 1970s, but crashed to pre-1960 levels in the early 1990s.

Beginning as a self-help programme in the mid-1960s, the Cotton Research and Promotion Programme was organized by U.S. cotton producers in response to cotton's steady decline in market share. At that time, producers voted to set up a per-bale assessment system to fund the programme, with built-in safeguards to protect their investments. With the passage of the Cotton Research and Promotion Act of 1966, the programme joined forces and began battling synthetic competitors and re-establishing markets for cotton. Today, the success of this programme has made cotton the best-selling fiber in the U.S. and one of the best-selling fibers in the world.

Administered by the Cotton Board and conducted by Cotton Incorporated, the Cotton Research and Promotion Programme works to greatly increase the demand for and profitability of cotton through various research and promotion activities. It is funded by U.S. cotton producers and importers used to make blue jeans; chambray, popularly used in the manufacture of blue work shirts (from which we get the term 'blue-collar'); and corduroy, seersucker, and cotton twill. Socks, underwear, and most T-shirts are made from cotton. Bed sheets often are made from cotton. Cotton also is used to make yarn used in crochet and knitting. Fabric also can be made from recycled or recovered cotton that otherwise would be thrown away during the spinning, weaving, or cutting process. While many fabrics are made completely of cotton, some materials blend cotton with other fibers, including rayon and synthetic fibers such as polyester. It can either be used in knitted or woven fabrics, as it can be blended with elastine to make a stretchier thread for knitted fabrics, and things such as stretch jeans.

In addition to the textile industry, cotton is in fishnets, coffee filters, tents, gunpowder cotton paper, and in bookbinding. The first Chinese paper was made of cotton fiber. Fire hoses were once made of cotton.

The cottonseed which remains after the cotton is ginned is used to produce cottonseed oil, which, after refining, can be consumed by humans like any other vegetable oil. The cottonseed meal that is left generally is fed to ruminant livestock; the gossypol remaining in the meal is toxic to mongastric animals. Cottonseed hulls can be added to dairy cattle rations for roughage. During the American slavery period, cotton root bark was used in a folk remedy as an abortifacient, that is, to provoke abortion.

Cotton linters are fine, silky fibers which adhere to the seeds of the cotton plant after ginning. These curly fibers typically are less than 1/8 in (3 mm) long. The term also may apply to the longer textile fiber staple lint as well as the shorter fuzzy fibers from some upland species. Linters are traditionally used in the manufacture of paper and as a raw material in the manufacture of cellulose.

Shiny cotton is a processed version of the fiber that can be made into cloth resembling satin for shirts and suits.

However, its hydrophobic property of not easily taking up water makes it unfit for the purpose of bath and dish towels (although examples of these made from shiny cotton are seen).

The term Egyptian cotton refers to the extra long staple cotton grown in Egypt and favoured for the luxury and upmarket brands worldwide. During the U.S. Civil War, with heavy European investments, Egyptian-grown cotton became a major alternate source for British textile mills. Egyptian cotton is more durable and softer than American Pima cotton, which is why it is more expensive. Pima cotton is American cotton that is grown in the southwestern states of the U.S.

The United States, with sales of $4.9 billion, and Africa, with sales of $2.1 billion, are the largest exporters of raw cotton. Total international trade is $12 billion. Africa's share of the cotton trade has doubled since 1980. Neither area has a significant domestic textile industry, textile manufacturing having moved to developing nations in Eastern and South Asia such as India and China. In Africa cotton is grown by numerous small holders. Dunavant Enterprises, based in Memphis, Tennessee, is the leading cotton broker in Africa with hundreds of purchasing agents. It operates cotton gins in Uganda, Mozambique, and Zambia. In Zambia it often offers loans for seed and expenses to the 180,000 small farmers who grow cotton for it, as well as advice on farming methods. Cargill also purchases cotton in Africa for export.

The 25,000 cotton growers in the United States are heavily subsidized at the rate of $2 billion per year. The future of these subsidies is uncertain and has led to anticipatory expansion of cotton brokers' operations in Africa. Dunavant expanded in Africa by buying out local operations. This is only possible in former British colonies and Mozambique; former French colonies continue to maintain tight monopolies, inherited from their former colonialist masters, on cotton purchases at low fixed prices.

In addition to concerns over subsidies, the cotton industries of some countries are criticized for employing child labour and damaging workers' health by exposure to pesticides used in production. The international production and trade situation has led to 'fair trade' cotton clothing and footwear, joining a rapidly growing market for organic clothing, fair fashion or so-called 'ethical fashion'. The fair trade system was initiated in 2005 with producers from Cameroon, Mali and Senegal.

Index

L

M

N

O

P

R

S

T

U

V

W

Z